LETTERS TO THE HON'BLE PRIME MINISTER

PART VIII

(THE BOOK IS A THINK-TANK, COMPRISING OF INNOVATIVE ORIGINAL CONCEPTS OF AUTHOR, THE ORIGINAL THINKER OVER SUGGESTION FOR MAKING BHARAT A DEVELOPED COUNTRY AND ACHIEVING GLOBAL PEACE.)

Dr. Nanda Nandan Das

NOTION PRESS

NOTION PRESS

India. Singapore. Malaysia.

Author:

DR. NANDA NANDAN DAS, Original Thinker
D. Sc, D. Litt, PDF (South Korea), PhD (Road), PhD (Building),
M.S.W, B.Sc. (Engg.), LLB, F.I.E, M.I.R.C, M.I.B.C
Former Secretary, Works, Government of Odisha
Former Chairman, O.B & C.C
Chairman, People's Welfare Suggestion Forum
Ex-Chairman, Odisha Durneeti Sangharsa Mancha
Ex-Team Leader, Mott. Mac Donald
Ex-Consultant, POSCO-INDIA
Address:
Plot. No. 2024, Chintamaniswar Area, Bhubaneswar-751006,
Odisha, India Mob. +91-9437617604
E-mail: nandanandan_das@yahoo.com

Editor:
Er. Shree Nandan Das

Chief Editor:
Prof. Purnima Mitra
First Edition: 2024

Dedicated to
Entire Global Family to live in PEACE in
Esteemed Mother Earth

CONTENTS

THE AUTHOR'S VIEW

The contents of this book are a compilation of my suggestions to the Hon'ble Prime Minister of India, focusing on various strategies for the nation's development. I firmly believe that all humanity is one family, united under the care of Mother Earth, irrespective of nationality or identity. As inhabitants of this shared planet, it is our collective duty to strive for harmony and well-being. My contributions to the United Nations reflect my unwavering commitment to achieving global peace.

Every concept presented in this book is original, born from spontaneous moments of inspiration, often at the most unusual hours. These ideas were later developed into articles and, following rigorous discussions with experts, were shared with the Hon'ble Prime Minister and other relevant authorities. My work is also documented in nine volumes titled Letters to the Hon'ble Prime Minister, which are available online. These volumes address critical challenges facing the country and propose pathways to global harmony. I am confident that if any developing or underdeveloped nation adopts these principles with sincerity, they will experience significant progress.

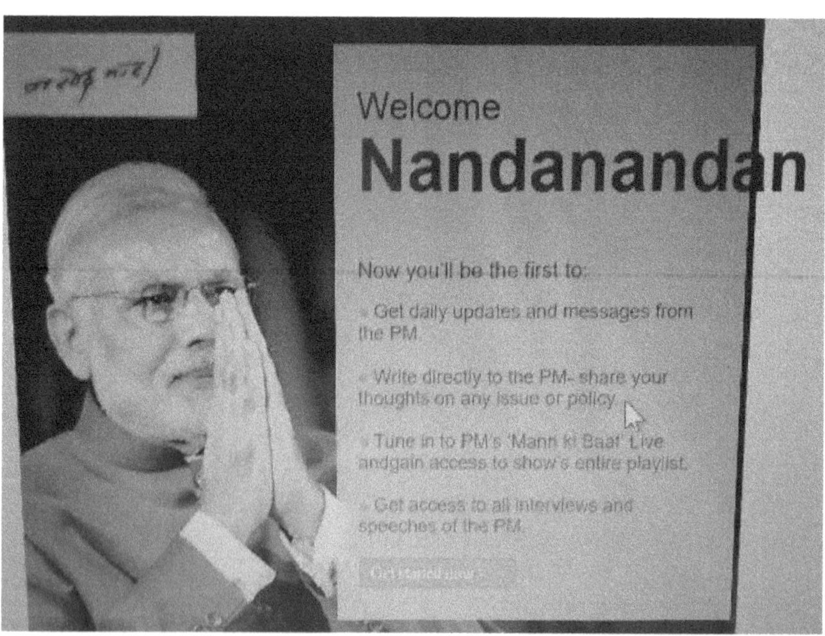

One of the defining moments in my journey was the warm reception I received from the Hon'ble Prime Minister of Bharat, Shri Narendra Modi Ji, in 2019. It fills me with immense satisfaction to see many of my ideas reflected in his speeches at the United Nations and in the Indian Parliament.

सत्यमेव जयते

प्रधान मंत्री
Prime Minister

New Delhi
आश्विन 12, शक संवत् 1946
04 October, 2024

Shri Nanda Nandan Das Ji,

Heartfelt gratitude to you for sending warm birthday wishes. I am overwhelmed to receive greetings from my family members such as yourself from across the country.

Your trust, support and cooperation are my real treasure. Your affectionate words fill me with new energy to strive in service of the nation. In the third term of our government, my resolve to fulfil the aspirations of the people and take India to great heights of progress has further strengthened.

Powered by the ability of our people and the skills of our youth, we have been setting new benchmarks in development over the last 10 years. *Amrit Kaal* is an opportunity to scale up our efforts to build a developed, inclusive and self-reliant nation.

The contribution of every Indian towards the progress of the nation is deeply valued.

With best wishes for your good health, happiness and prosperity.

Yours,

(Narendra Modi)

Shri Nanda Nandan Das
Plot- 2024, Chintamaniswar Area
Bhubaneswar, District- Khordha
Odisha- 751006

vii

One cherished memory is a letter I received from the Hon'ble Prime Minister dated October 4, 2024. It stands as a source of immense pride not only for me but also for my family and community. The Hon'ble Prime Minister's words, "Your trust, support, and cooperation are my real treasure. Your affectionate words fill me with new energy to strive in service of the nation. In the third term of our government, my resolve to fulfil the aspirations of the people and take India to great heights of progress has further strengthened," left me overwhelmed and deeply moved. I feel profound gratitude for such an encouraging acknowledgment.

This journey of contributing to the nation's growth and vision has been both humbling and fulfilling. I hope my work continues to inspire progress, unity, and peace for all.

Beyond these contributions, I have also made discoveries related to fundamental aspects of Earth sciences, including the Earth's rotation on its axis in an anti-clockwise direction (resulting in day and night), the Moon's revolution around the Earth over a month, and the existence of the Earth's magnetic field. These findings were communicated to ISRO and the Hon'ble Prime Minister as evidence of my dedication to advancing knowledge.

Dr. Nanda Nandan Das, Original Thinker,
The Author

EDITORIAL DESK

Dr. Nanda Nandan Das, born on December 21, 1943, in the village of Baudpur, Bhadrak, Odisha, Bharat, is a distinguished figure in the realm of engineering and administrative services. He embarked on his professional journey diligently after obtaining a BSc in Engineering from UCE, Burla, in 1965. His illustrious career culminated in a more sharpened manner when he got retired as the Secretary of Works Govt. of Odisha and Chairman of O.B & C.C. on December 31, 2001. His unwavering dedication towards his duty and innovative problem-solving abilities made him a trailblazer, consistently demonstrating that nothing is insurmountable.

Recognition and accolades have followed Dr. Nanda Nandan Das throughout his career:

State Awards: Six prestigious honours from "The Institution of Engineers India, Odisha Centre, Bhubaneswar" in 2002, 2003, 2004, 2006, 2016, and 2017.

National Recognition: Rashtriya Gourav Award - Certificate of Excellence presented by Dr. G.V.G. Krishnamurty, the Honourable Former Election Commissioner, in 2004.

International Acknowledgment: PDF, South Korea, recognized Dr. Nanda Nandan Das's contributions in 2016.

- Gopabandhu Das Samman in 2019
- Madhusudan Das Samman in 2020.
- Original Thinker Award in 2018.
- Lifetime Achievement Award from 'The Institution of Engineers India, Odisha Centre' in 2013.
- Felicitation by ISTE, Odisha Section, in 2017.

Dr. Nanda Nandan Das's remarkable achievements extend beyond his professional life.

- ➤ Being a confident swimmer, he saves four lives from perilous situations in rivers like the Ganges, Salandi, and Indravati.
- ➤ His globetrotting experiences have taken him to numerous countries, including Britain, Paris, Germany, Italy, Switzerland,

Liechtenstein, Netherlands, Belgium, Austria, Vatican, USA, Canada, Dubai, Abu Dhabi, Malaysia, Australia, New Zealand, Fiji, China, Japan, Thailand, South Africa, Singapore, Nepal, and Sri Lanka.

➢ In the realm of scientific discovery, Dr. Nanda Nandan Das stands as a pioneer.

   i.   He proposed a ground breaking theory on the Earth's rotation on its axis, resulting in day and night, as well as the Moon's revolution around the Earth, leading to the concept of a month.

   ii. His innovative concept of the existence of a magnetic field in Earth due to the rotation of Earth on its axis, a thought-provoking mystery, has been sent to ISRO and Hon'ble Prime Minister, India.

These discoveries have been referred to ISRO and Hon'ble Prime Minister, India

Dr. Nanda Nandan Das's literary contributions are equally noteworthy, with 15 published books to his name. Notable works include "Letters to the Hon'ble Prime Minister"(nine volumes), which delves into administrative reforms in Bharat. If any developing/under-developed country would follow these innovative concepts sincerely, then it would be developed soon. His book 'Global Peace', was sent to the Presidents/ Prime Ministers of about 170 countries during 2017. This effort led to significant diplomatic developments, including the meeting between the Presidents of America and North Korea in Singapore on June 12, 2018, on 'Global Peace'.

Dr. Nanda Nandan Das's devotion to social causes is also evident. He proposed the implementation of the Indian Citizenship Card to the Ministry of Home Affairs in 2009, a concept that later evolved into the Aadhaar Card. Keeping him isolated with undisturbed mind, he tirelessly suggests innovative ideas to the Honourable Prime Minister of Bharat to create a crime and poverty free nation. Additionally, he advocates for the inclusion of Moral Science, (Already suggested the course from class 1 to graduation, based on all being ideal Indians and how to make the country developed) in educational curriculum for the reformation of the country.

Dr. Nanda Nandan Das's ultimate aim is to foster patriotism, ingenuity, quality, and moral values among citizens, both in Bharat and globally.

He envisions a world where countries function as a united family, and "Religion Humanity" takes precedence over any religious divide.

Throughout his tenure, Dr. Nanda Nandan Das initiated successful projects, such as installing statues of deities in government buildings to prevent spitting on the walls, hindering unhygienic and disrespectful attitudes. His dedication to service has been recognized by the national daily, The Hindustan Times, during 2002, among others.

His entry in Universe, Earth, Country, State, District, Village:

1.   The Universe: - Rotation of Earth on its axis forming day & night, existence of magnetic field on Earth, the causes still remain a mystery, but have been discovered by Dr. Das.

2.   The Earth: His book GLOBAL PEACE had been sent to heads of 170 countries achieving peace globally.

3.   The Country: He initiated to introduce Indian ID card during 2009, and the outcome is the Aadhaar Card. Due to the inspiration of PM, Dr. Das suggested many issues, which are included in 9 books of 'Letters to the Hon'ble Prime Minister'. Available-
Amazon and Flipkart.

4.   The State: The OVERDRAFT of the state has been stopped due to his suggestion to the finance minister during 2005. Best Engineer of the state, is being awarded 'Dr. Nanda Nandan Das Award' every year by Institution of Engineers, India, Bhubaneswar.

5.   The district: -He developed roads, constructed new Rajghat Bridge, renovated some high schools.

6.   The Village: He developed road, school, and Pravat Club.

This book 'Letters to the Hon'ble Prime Minister' is a reservoir of instant solutions and a comprehensive encyclopaedia dedicated to our beloved Motherland, Bharat.

Prof. Purnima Mitra,
The Chief Editor,
Asst. Professor,
NIIS Group of Institutions

CHAPTER I

WELFARE OF ENTIRE HUMAN FAMILIES OF EARTH

Due to the unrest caused by the repeated wars (World War I and World War II) and the devastation of Japan by atomic bombings in 1945, an international peace committee was formed on October 24, 1945, known as the United Nations (UN). The UN was established to promote global peace. On December 16, 2021, a proposal titled "Path to Global Peace" was submitted to the UN Security Council (UNSC). However, it has been observed that the peace efforts have been undermined by some countries with veto power, leading to the encouragement of war, terrorism, and crime, while disregarding humanity.

The current G20, which comprises 21 countries, including those with veto power, received a proposal for the welfare of the entire human family on October 10, 2023. The G20 is suggested to function like the UN and take steps to promote global peace based on the principle of "One Earth, One Family, One Future."

REGISTRATION NUMBER: PMOPG/E/2023/0214637
Dt. 10.10.2023

To
The Hon'ble President G 20.
Through Special Secretary, G 20
Sub-Welfare of entire Human Family of Earth.
Respected Sir,
It is observed that Palestine has attacked Israel recently, and there is a huge loss of lives and properties. UNO is not functioning as per verdicts for peace of 24.10.1945. The veto power is being miss-utilized. It was expected that since then, human beings gradually got more civilized, they would understand the actual truth of human lives and would plan the living of entire mankind in a better way. All human beings are born free on Earth like other living beings, and departing from Earth is a must for all, irrespective of ages, religions, castes, countries' heads, terrorists, and common people. The human beings were wild and nomads, but then they

became gradually civilized. They started to settle, created religions, different border lines, zonal feelings, and so on in the course of time, unlike other living beings. As we accept elephants, tigers, etc. all living beings should live well. So, human beings should also live well within short living even if it is a hundred years. I have already indicated it in registration number: PMOPG/E/ 2023/0181196, Dt. 10.09.2023 to include peace for the entire mankind of the Mother Earth in G 20.

The present war between Israel and Palestine, Russia & Ukraine and lots of all time continuing disputes between many countries, involve huge expenditure in defence and enmity among countries and the people, which hamper wellbeing of their own citizens. The terrorists are wild animals in human look, such activities must be wiped out by any means. The egoism, expansionism, and self-centeredness among the heads of some countries are undesirable. All must keep in mind that they would do well for all human beings, neighbouring countries before they depart from the Earth. They should not be defamed like Hitler in history. All countries' heads should express in G 20, how they can do good for all and helpful to other countries to maintain the principle "One Earth, One Family and one Future." G 20 should also function in UNO.

With thanks,

Yours sincerely,

Dr. Nanda Nandan Das, Original Thinker,

Former Secretary, Works, Govt. of Odisha.

Former Chairman, O. B & C. C

Chairman, People's Welfare Suggestion Forum

Former Chairman, Odisha Durneeti Sangharsh Mancha

Dt 10.10.2023

CHAPTER II

GENERATING NATIONALISM AS ALL ARE IDEAL BHARATIYA-A MEANS TO ACHIEVE CRIME & POVERTY FREE COUNTRY.

Grievance is registered successfully.
Registration Number: PMOPG/E/2023/0208018

Dt. 5.10.2023
Respected Shri Narendra Modi Ji, Hon'ble PM, Bharat.

1) Earth is the place for human beings, like other living beings. The religions, castes, different countries' borders, zonal feelings, etc. were created after the human mass became civilized. All the citizens of our country are Bharatiya by birth. Priority on 'Country First' and feeling as Bharatiya should be generated among all through education, multimedia, and enforcement of law. In Japan, the most insulting remark for one Japanese is if one says 'you are not Japanese'. Due to such a national feeling, countries like Japan, Sweden, Finland, Norway, etc. are developed.

2) Now, some political parties create narrow feelings, citing differences of castes among the citizens to gain a vote bank. After independence, the constitution was formed, and the quota system was provided for 10 years, but such a quota system is still lingering. The quota is mostly availed by creamy class people of the same category, so the BPL persons are deprived of such relief. These creamy classes never want to uplift their BPL categories so as to linger such a quota system for enjoying such benefit. It is noticed that no party gives emphasize on the issue on political interest, which restricts to raising BPL status.

Since it is not possible to wave out quota systems easily, policy should be made to continue the quota system for 5 years, ignoring the creamy classes of the same category. There would be two classes, i.e. rich & poor, which covers all classes.

3) Prime Minister, Sir, your effort to uplift the poverty line by various activities is praise worthy. In fact, some efforts are not reaching among common mass. Out of lots, I like to cite some examples, i.e. Atal-Pension Yojana, PMSBY, PMJJBY are still unknown to majority of citizens in the country. So, within 9 years many have been debarred of getting such facility. This is because the parties in power in the states avoid on such matter in order to lose vote bank. So, proper action should be taken to involve all through door to door canvasing and the right administration.

4) There should not be any political parties on religious and caste basis. In fact, all Bharatiya in our country are the same. A schedule tribe can be here President. Schedule caste becomes IAS, and OBC becomes Prime Minister. So, there should be only relief to be proved to all BPL.

5) Each religious person can observe religion in one's own house and in the institution without disturbing others. Any function that involves mass gathering, prior permission should be taken from government or there should be standing instruction from govt. to avoid religious disputes.

6) Our country Bharat is mostly Sanatan Dharma - Hindu since long. Mostly Jain, Buddha, Sikh are different wings of the Hindu religion. The concept of Sanatan Dharma is 'Vasudhaiva Kutumbakam' & 'Sarbe Bhabantu Sukhinnah'-it means all are one family of Earth and all live well. Such versions mean peace on Earth. On different times, some invaders of different religions have conquered and settled here. All religious institutions should be properly maintained, but damage to any institution by other religious invaders and terrorists are to be restored, and heritage of the nation must be maintained to encourage tourism.

FINAL FINDINGS:

1. The top priority on all is Bharatiya i.e. nationalism. Others are secondary with self-interest.
2. All programming should be made to raise the financial status of economically backward classes with solving unemployment problems.
3. All schemes of Centre govt. for welfare of the common citizens, should reach to each and all by proper administration.
4. There should not be any political party on caste and religion basis.
5. There should not be any religious disputes.
6. All old religious institutions should be properly maintained. The heritage of Bharat should be restored, which were damaged by terrorist and invaders.

Regards,

Yours sincerely,

Dr Nanda Nandan Das, Original Thinker

Dt. 5.10.2023

Current Status-Case closed

Date of Action-10/10/2023

Reason-Others

Remark-General comments

Rating-Average

Rating Remarks-Not Satisfied

Rating

☆☆☆☆☆ Average

Rating Remarks

NotSatisfied

CHAPTER III

SUGGESTION TO MAKE PROMPTNESS IN POSTAL DEPARTMENT

Grievance is registered successfully.
Registration Number: PMOPG/E/2023/0215505
Dt. 11.10.2023.
Dt. 09.10.2023
Respected Shri Narendra Modi Ji, Hon'ble Prime Minister, India I like to put here the harassment done to customers by the Postal Department. A Postal NSC had got matured on July 2023, and the postal agent told me to sign the NSC before the concerned officer in person as this requisite had been in recent order. I am very old and was unable to go to the post office during July. Today however, by any means I appeared before APM, Suresh Khuntia of Chief PMG, Odisha, Bhubaneswar. I enquired that for 30 years matters concerned to post office are dealt by the concerned agent, but why it is required to appear personally for a signature to credit the amount to my SB account (not connected to transaction of cash). The APM told me to contact DPM on such matter. So, I contacted DPM. He said that this is a recent order.

I told the gentleman that our country has advanced much and has secured a top position in the world. Even vehicles aren't being detained in toll gate transacting toll through Fast tag, and the transaction of money through UPI is a common means in the country. *The postal department is still in stone-age and trying to get fire by striking two stones.* This is a common practice to harass customers in different transactions. Postal Department is a very old organization, and their process of work style is very slow, delayed, and careless towards the public all the time. It is requested to issue proper direction to the department for having prompt action on each transaction, with good dealing with costumers and senior citizens.

With heartiest regards,
Yours sincerely.
Dr. Nanda Nandan Das, Original Thinker,
Former Secretary, Works, Govt. of Odisha.
Former Chairman, OB&CC
Chairman, People's Welfare Suggestion Forum
Former Chairman, Odisha Durneeti Sangharsa Mancha
Dt. 09.10.2023

Date of receipt -11.10.2023
Current Status-Case closed
Date of Action-12/10/2023
Remarks-There is no provision made for messenger in the forms notified by the Ministry of Finance in GSPR 2018 and in various National Savings Schemes 2019. As per the provisions under Rule 12 of GSPR 2018, no messenger is allowed for any type of payment viz. maturity proceeds, partial withdrawal or interest. However, keeping in view of difficulties faced by the Senior Citizens or people suffering with illness, the issue was taken up with Ministry of Finance and keeping the provisions in Rule 11 of Government Savings Promotion General Rules-2018 in mind, competent authority has decided that in case of extreme exigencies (i.e. Senior Citizens or illness of account holder or suffering from physical infirmity or is with differently-abled conditions) the withdrawal or loan or account closure or premature closure may be allowed through authorized person with prescribed terms and conditions. The case is closed accordingly.
Officer Concerns to Officer Name:
Ms. Suchismita Swain (DPS Headquarters)
Organisation Name: Orissa Postal Circle
Contact Address:
Office of the CPMG, Odisha Circle, Bhubaneswar, Odisha

TO MAKE PROMPTNESS IN POSTAL DEPARTMENT

Email Address: cpmg_ori@indiapost.gov.in
Contact Number: 06742391426

THE COMMENT ON THE REMARK TO PMO OVER PHONE-
This comment is voice recorded for action over it in higher level.

I am of age 80, not able to move. On personal appearance before the APM, on 09.10.2023 the NSC matured amount has already been credited to the SB account. I am citing here some examples for facility of common mass. Anybody sign on any one's matured FD, mentioning the amount to be credited to SB account in banking system and it is done so, without personal appearance of the depositor. The same procedure may be adopted in Postal Department for costumer's convenience, as it is not cash transaction. Our country is advancing fast, UPI transaction, fast tag transaction in toll gate and many more transactions in banking system have been modernized for convenience of costumers, prompt action, without loss of time. So Postal Department should revise age-old rules to make modernize in part with present era for prompt action, convenience to public. This will not only bring reliability on Postal service but also increase financial transaction.
Thanks,
Dr. Nanda Nandan Das, Original Thinker,
Date- 13.10.2023
This has been told over phone to the person concerned of PMO at 2pm on 13.10.2023.
My rating is good.
Dr. Nanda Nandan Das

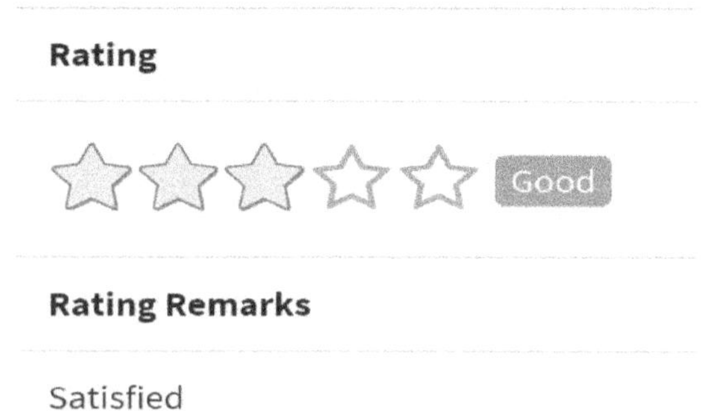

NANDANANDAN DAS <nandanandan_das@yahoo.com>
To: cpmg_ori@indiapost.gov.in, nandanandan_das@yahoo.com
Fri, Oct 13 at 7:20 PM
Dt. 13.10.2023
Dear Sir/Madam,
My postal transaction was made on 09.10.2023, I suggested to Hon'ble Prime Minister on 11.10.2023 over the matter and creation of problems. It was considered and closed on 12.10.2023 in PMO. It was communicated for my rating over the remark by postal department on 13.10.2023 through phone by direct contact. This is what the prompt action of PMO of present Bharat, as on today. The total transaction over the matter is attached herewith for your information. It is requested to be very particular for prompt actions and dealings with the costumers in the postal department to match with the desire of Hon'ble Prime Minister, Bharat, Shri Narendra Modi Ji, by means of modernized technology. This will increase reliability of the costumers and raise financial dealings in the department, by reformation of rule as suitable. With regards,
Yours sincerely,
DR. Nanda Nandan Das, Original Thinker,
Former Secretary, Works, Govt. of Odisha.
Former Chairman, O. B & C. C
Chairman, People's Welfare Suggestion
Forum
Former Chairman, Odisha Durneeti Sangharsa
Mancha
Ex-Team Leader, Mott. Mac Donald
Ex-Consultant, POSCO-INDIA

CHAPTER IV

AN AWARENESS ON DEFENCE POLICIES

Registration Number: PMOPG/E/2023/0249414
Dt. 24.11.2023
Respected Shri Narendra Modi Ji, Hon'ble Prime Minister, India.
It is noticed that the staff of Pakistan Military maintain wealthy status by various unfair means. They don't want to spare their military personnel to die by going directly against India. Therefore, they have created terrorists to create problem in India by which the defence personnel, police, and civilians of our country are killed, and properties get destroyed. These terrorists are spared to be killed without hampering their own military personnel. Such tricks of Pakistan should be known and may be planned to be dealt with accordingly.
With heartiest regards,
Yours sincerely,
Dr. Nanda Nandan Das, Original Thinker
Former Secretary, Works,
Chairman, **Description**
Dt. 24.11.2023
Current Status-Case closed
Date of Action-25/11/2023
Remarks-GEN. COMMENTS NOT CONTAINING SPECIFIC GRIEVANCE
Rating-Very Good
Rating Remarks-
Satisfied
People's Welfare Suggestion Forum.
Dt. 24.11.2023

CHAPTER V

ASSURED ANIMAL FREE ROAD ON ROAD

The Grievance is registered successfully.
Registration Number: PMOPG/E/2023/0179640
Dt. 07. 09.2023

Respected Shri Narendra Modi Ji, Hon'ble Prime Minister, India

It is learned from the 'TIMES NOW NAV BHARAT TV' on 06.09.2023 that there are severe injuries and loss of lives due to attack and dashing of stray bulls, dogs, cows, goats etc. on the road. There are a lot of deaths due to rabies. At the same time, there are deaths of such animals on the road due to accidents. No such movement of animals is allowed in any developed country. Our country is no longer an uncivilized and undeveloped country. Since our country is progressing fast, it is necessary to make the roads free from movements/entry of animals. Let the pedestrians and traffics move freely on the road without such risk. It is expected that all steps should be taken to keep the roads free from these animals before the G-20 Summit, which is scheduled on the 9th and 10th of this month. To stop the entry of any animal on the road should be continued there after strictly. Following steps should be taken to make the roads free of animals:

1.   Dogs

•   The pet dogs should be kept by the owners in their houses, making them registered. Free movement of these dogs on the road or taking these dogs on the road by owners for leaving excreta should be banned strictly. In San-Francisco, America, one place, close to the Pacific Ocean, is kept as Dog-Park. The dogs are brought there for their recreation purpose. It is astonishing to find that no dog creates any foul there, as the dogs are trained to use their toilets in their respective houses. Such awareness should be generated among the citizens.

• The entry of street dogs to the road or moving freely in the village or in urban areas should strictly be stopped. The disposal of such dogs is the matter of government administration.

2. Cattle- The cows, oxen, buffalos, bulls, pigs, etc. should be restricted to get entry to the roads. These cattle, even poultry, should not be allowed to stay inside the urban and village areas, as they create an unhygienic atmosphere in the locality. Either these should be kept far away from the locality on their own or on a cooperative basis. No way, the bulls create havoc on the road, if require, these may be turned to ox as usual. I have got such experience to find the cattle, kept away from the locality while moving from Las Vegas to San Francisco.

Some NGOs keep sympathy for these animals. They can be allowed to keep such animals in their own custody, but should put a burden over others. Death, due to an accident of any animal on the road, should not be held responsible upon the driver.

I have already suggested earlier on the matter. Such banning to entry of animals on road has been a major point, published in IRC magazine on the subject 'Control of Road Accident' by me as the author during August 2013.

It is requested to consider such vital issues, which is definitely a part of the means of development of the country. With heartiest regards,

Yours sincerely,

Dr. Nanda Nandan Das, Original Thinker

Former Secretary, Works, Odisha

Chairman, People's Welfare Suggestion Forum.

Former Chairman, OB&CC

Dt. 07.09.2023

NARENDRA MODI, PRIME MINISTER, INDIA

Date of Receipt-07/09/2023
Received By Ministry/Department-Prime Minister's Office
Grievance Description-
Current Status-Case closed
Date of Action-20/09/2023
Remarks-The AWBI is a statutory body enacted under Prevention of Cruelty to Animal Act 1960. The local authorities are responsible for taking care of the stray animals in those areas. The law enforcement is carried out by the law enforcement of the concerned State Governments and UTs. As per section 3 and section 11 1 of the prevention of cruelty to animal act, 1960 it is an offense if an animal is subjected to unnecessary pain or suffering. The board has already brought the directions of the Hon'ble supreme court in its order dated 7.5.2014 for compliance of law enforcement authorities for taking necessary action in the matter to prevent unnecessary pain or suffering to animals and also issued several advisories and circulars regarding the stray animals vide letter dated 12th July, 2018 and 27th February, 2020 and the same is available in website www.awbi.gov.in The matter may be taken up with the concerned local bodies for taking further appropriate action.

Officer Concerns to Officer Name-Shri G.N. Singh (Joint Secretary GC)
Organisation Name-Department of Animal Husbandry, Dairying
Contact Address-Room No. 248C, 2nd Floor, Krishi Bhavan New Delhi
Email Address-gn.singh13@nic.in
Contact Number-01123389620

My comment on the disposal of the issue is as follow:

PMO registration number: PMOPG/E/2023/0179640

ASSURED ANIMAL FREE ROAD

Dt. 20/09/2023

I am not satisfied on the remark. There is no solution on the issue. The matter is to keep roads free of entry of animals for safety of lives and property of human beings as well as safety against injury and death of animals by accidents. It is not concerned to any cruelty to animals, rather concerned to safety of animals. It is not a local or state matter rather, it is a national issue. Government is to find the means to tackle such situation without cruelty to animals. I have suggested some solutions for safety of animals citing some examples in some developed countries. It is not concerned to a single department. All concerned departments cooperatively should find out the solution over such critical issue and make the roads free of animals.

Dr. Nanda Nandan Das, Original Thinker
Former Secretary, Works, Odisha
Chairman, People's Welfare Suggestion Forum.
Former Chairman, OB&CC

प्रशासनिक सुधार और लोक शिकायत विभाग

DEPARTMENT OF

ADMINISTRATIVE REFORMS
& PUBLIC GRIEVANCES

सत्यमेव जयते

Dt. 20/09/2023

Received By Ministry/Department-Prime Minister's Office
GRIEVANCE DESCRIPTION:
Dt.20.09.2023
Respected Shri Narendra Modi Ji, Hon'ble PM, Bharat, The case is closed over the registration number PMOPG/E/2023/0179640 on 20.09.2023 with the remark: The AWBI is a statutory body enacted under Prevention of Cruelty to Animal Act 1960. The local authorities are responsible for taking care of the stray animals in

those areas. The law enforcement is carried out by the law enforcement of the concerned State Governments and UTs. As per section 3 and section 11 1 of the prevention of cruelty to animal act, 1960 it is an offense if an animal is subjected to unnecessary pain or suffering. The board has already brought the directions of the Hon'ble supreme court in its order dated 7.5.2014 for compliance of law enforcement authorities for taking necessary action in the matter to prevent unnecessary pain or suffering to animals and also issued several advisories and circulars regarding the stray animals vide letter dated 12th July, 2018 and 27th February, 2020 and the same is available in website www.awbi.gov.in The matter may be taken up with the concerned local bodies for taking action. My comment over the disposal of the issue is as follow: I am not satisfied on the remark. There is no solution on the remark. The matter is to keep roads free of entry of animals for safety of lives and property of human beings as well as safety against injury and death of animals by accidents. It is not concerned to any cruelty to animal, rather concerned to safety of animals. It is not a local or state matter rather, it is a national issue. The entries of animals to road were restricted during G20 Session also. Government is to find the means to tackle such situation. I have suggested solutions for safety of animals citing some examples of some developed countries. It is not concerned to a single department like Organization Name-Department of Animal Husbandry, Dairying. Rather Road and Transport department should initiate on the issue and get the roads animals free after contacting all concerned departments cooperatively.

With heartiest regards,
Yours sincerely,
Nanda Nandan Das, Original Thinker
Chairman, People's Welfare Suggestion Forum.
Dt. 20.09.2023

Current Status-Case closed
Date of Action-16/10/2023
Remarks-

The AWBI is a statutory body enacted under Prevention of Cruelty to Animal Act 1960. The local authorities are responsible for taking care of the stray animals in those areas. The law enforcement is carried out by the law enforcement of the

Rating

★☆☆☆☆ Poor

Rating Remarks

NotSatisfied

concerned State Governments and UTs. As per section 3 and section 11 1 of the prevention of cruelty to animal act, 1960 it is an offense if an animal is subjected to unnecessary pain or suffering. The board has already brought the directions of the Hon'ble supreme court in its order dated 7.5.2014 for compliance of law enforcement authorities for taking necessary action in the matter to prevent unnecessary pain or suffering to animals and also issued several advisories and circulars regarding the stray animals vide letter dated 12th July, 2018 and 27th February, 2020 and the same is available in website www.awbi.gov.in The matter may be taken up with the concerned local bodies for taking further appropriate action. Further to the above, it is the responsibility of the local bodies to see that the stray animals except stray dogs are taken care properly and they are sheltered. The Member Secretary, Odisha Animal Welfare Board, office of the Directorate of the Department of Animal Husbandry may be contacted for further appropriate action.

Rating-Poor

Rating Remarks: Not Satisfied

Appeal Details

Appeal Number-DOAHD/C/A/23/0000065

Date of Receipt-16/10/2023

Appeal Text-Not Satisfied

Current Status-Appeal Received

Officer Concerns to Officer Name

Shri G.N. Singh (Joint Secretary GC)

Organisation name-Department of Animal Husbandry, Dairying

Contact Address-Room No. 248C, 2nd Floor, Krishi Bhavan New Delhi

Email Address-gn.singh13@nic.in

Contact Number-01123389620

CHAPTER VI

SOLUTION TO BORDER DISPUTES OF ODISHA AND OTHER STATES IN A TARGETED TIME

Your Grievance is registered successfully.
Registration Number: PMOPG/E/2024/0025069
Dt. 01.02.2024

Respected Shri Narendra Modi Ji, Hon'ble Prime Minister, India.

It is regarding solution to inter-state border disputes in the country. There was discussion in 93rd webinar of Thinker's Club over the solution to disputes among the State of Odisha and its neighbouring states. It was decided that since these are national issues, the matter may be referred to the Hon'ble Prime Minister, India for taking further action over the matter centrally. The concluding script of webinar is attached separately for favour of kind perusal and action. With Heartiest regards,

Yours sincerely,

Dr. Nanda Nandan Das, Original Thinker,

Chairman, People's Welfare Suggestion Forum.

Dt. 01.02.2024

Current Status-Case closed **Date of Action-**
26/02/2024

Remarks-Suggestion Noted

Officer NameG. Parthasarthi (Joint Secretary CS)

Organisation name-CS Division

Address-MDCNSNEW DELHI

MINUTES OF DISCUSSION OF 93rd WEBINAR OF THINKER'S CLUB:

There were 93 webinars by Thinker's Club on border issue of Odisha on 22.12.2023. Shri Barada Prasanna Das, President Thinker' Club presided the webinar. The efforts taken for clearance of disputes of Odisha with different bordering states, were explained by various speakers. Odisha became an independent state on 01.04.1936, but many border issues continue to linger since about nine decades. No doubt there was sincere effort from the Odisha Government and the local leaders forming different committees to finalize the disputes, but the problems remain unsolved till date. The speakers expressed the critical border issues, which were suggested to the government. Although the Odisha Government has taken steps on various issues, the problems remain unsolved.

Dr. Nanda Nandan Das, Original Thinker, Former Secretary Works, Chairman, People's Welfare Suggestion Forum, suggested some solutions to overcome the issues. Since the border issues of all the states are national problem, it is suggested to follow certain points to overcome the lingered problems:

'ସୀମା ବିବାଦ ତୁଟାନ୍ତୁ ସରକାର'

କଟକ,୨୪।୧୨(ବ୍ୟୁରୋ): ଓଡ଼ିଶା ସହ ଆନ୍ଧ୍ରପ୍ରଦେଶ, ପଶ୍ଚିମବଙ୍ଗ, ଛତିଶଗଡ଼ ଓ ଝାଡ଼ଖଣ୍ଡର ସୀମା ବିବାଦ ଲାଗିରହିଛି। ତେଣୁ ରାଜ୍ୟ ସରକାର ଏହି ବିବାଦର ସମାଧାନ କରନ୍ତୁ ବୋଲି ଥିଙ୍କର୍ସ କ୍ଲବର ୯୩ ତମ ୱେବିନାର ଆଲୋଚନାଚକ୍ରରେ ମତ ପ୍ରକାଶ ପାଇଛି। ସଭାପତି ବରଦ ଦାସଙ୍କ ଅଧ୍ୟକ୍ଷତାରେ ଅନୁଷ୍ଠିତ ଆଲୋଚନାଚକ୍ରରେ ଉତ୍କଳ ସମ୍ମିଳନୀ ସଭାପତି ଡ଼ଃ ଅଦ୍ୱୈତ କୁମାର ପାତ୍ର, ସାମ୍ବାଦିକ ଅବନି ନାଥ, ଡ଼ଃ ନନ୍ଦ ନନ୍ଦନ ଦାସ, ଜୟନ୍ତ ସାମଲ, ଦୁର୍ଗା ପାତ୍ର, ମନୋଜ ହୋତା, ଡ଼ଃ ମୃଷାଙ୍କ ପରିଡ଼ା, ଡ଼। ରଜତ ଶତପଥୀ, ସାଧାରଣ ବେହେରା, ସୁପେଶର ଘଣକାର ମିଶ୍ର, ରବୀନ୍ଦ୍ର କୁମାର ମିଶ୍ର ଓ ବିଭୁଦର ମହାନ୍ତି ଅଂଶଗ୍ରହଣ କରିଥିଲେ।

A 'National Border Conflict Board' (NBCB) may be formed nationally and 'Border Conflict Board' of all states may be created under NBCB. The state wise naming of the board would be according to the state. For e.g. Odisha Border Conflict Board (OBCB) for Odisha State.

The 'State Border Conflict Board' would associate with the leaders and committees of border dispute of state.

The border disputes may be due to local language & custom, availability of resources, scarcity of facility as minority and many such issues.

Proper consideration should be made to look after the facilities for minorities for the language in schooling, all other scopes.

As regarding availability of resources, the central government may take suitable steps in such a way so that both the states should be satisfied on the action.

Nothing is permanent for any one, the issue that has been lingering for decades is helpful for none, hampering both financially as well as socially in terms of time. Everything, in fact is national property.

Such Board of each state under the guidance of NBCB would take proper steps to solve all issues with

ଥିଙ୍କର୍ସ କ୍ଲବର ଆଭାସି ଆଲୋଚନାଚକ୍ର

କଟକ,୨୪ ।୧୨ : ଥିଙ୍କର୍ସ କ୍ଲବର ଆଭାସି ଆଲୋଚନାଚକ୍ର ସଭାପତି ବରଦାପ୍ରସନ୍ନ ଦାସଙ୍କ ଅଧ୍ୟକ୍ଷତାରେ ଅନୁଷ୍ଠିତ ହୋଇଯାଇଛି । ଆଲୋଚନାରେ ଉକ୍ଳ ସମ୍ମିଳନୀ ସଭାପତି ଡ.ଅଦ୍ୱୈତ କୁମାର ପାତ୍ର, ଅବନୀ ଚାନ୍ଦ, ଡ.ନନ୍ଦନନ୍ଦନ ଦାସ, ଜଗତ ସାମଲ, ଡ.ପୁଷ୍ପାଞ୍ଜଳି ପରିଡ଼ା, ଡ.ରଜତ ଶତପଥୀ, ପ୍ରଫେସର ଉମାଶଙ୍କର ମିଶ୍ର, ରବୀନ୍ଦ୍ର କୁମାର ମିଶ୍ର ଓ ବିଭୁଦତ୍ତ ମହାନ୍ତି ପ୍ରମୁଖ ଓଡ଼ିଶାର ସୀମା ବିବାଦର ସମାଧାନ କରିବାକୁ ସରକାର ଏକ ସ୍ୱତନ୍ତ୍ର ବିଭାଗ ସୃଷ୍ଟି କରିବାକୁ ନିବେଦନ କରିଥିଲେ । ଏହା ଆମର ଜାତୀୟ ସମସ୍ୟା ହୋଇଥିବାରୁ ପ୍ରଧାନମନ୍ତ୍ରୀଙ୍କ ଦୃଷ୍ଟି ଆକର୍ଷଣ କରିବେ ବୋଲି ଡ.ନନ୍ଦ ନନ୍ଦନ ଦାସ କହିଥିଲେ ।

guidance of NBCB would take proper steps to solve all issues with a targeted time say within one year. With such decision by centre, the border disputes would be solved forever. Such matter was published in the daily newspapers e.g. The Samaj and the Prameya. The English scripts are cited below.

The English script of news published in the newspaper Samaya 'GOVERNMENT SHOULD FINALIZE BORDER ISSUE SOON.

The 93rd webinar of Thinker Club, presided by Sri Barada Prasanna Das was held to decide border issue between Odisha and adjoining states such as Andhra Pradesh, Chhattisgarh, Jharkhand and West Bengal.

Dr. Aditya Kumar Patra, President of Utkal Sammilani, Media Person Abani Chand, Dr. Nanda Nandan Das, Durga Padhi, Manisha Tripathi, Jagat Samal, Dr. Puspanjali Parida, Dr. Rajat Satpathi, Prof. Umasankar Mishra, Rabindra Kumar Mishra, Bibhudutt Mohanty and many more participated in the session. They placed suitable reasons to finalize such long pending issues.

The English script of news published in the newspaper, The Samaj is 'DISCUSSION ON 93rd WEBINER, THINKER'S CLUB'

The webinar was presided by Shri Barada Prasanna Das, President Thinkr's Club. Dr Aditya Kumar Patra, President of Utkal Sammilani, Abani Chand, Dr. Nanda Nandan Das, Jagat Samal, Dr. Puspanjali Parida, Dr. Rajat Satpathi, Prof. Umasankar Mishra, Bibhudatt Mahanty and many more attended the session. They placed reasonable reasons for finalizing such long pending issues by forming special committee. Dr. Nanda Nandan Das expressed, these are national issues, since concerned to all the states of the country and it would be brought to lime light of Hon'ble Prime Mister, India.

It was decided in the webinar to communicate the matter to Hon'ble Prime Minister, India for taking an early step to overcome such issues in a stipulated scheduled time bound period.

Shri Barada Prasanna Das, President Thinker's Club

Ex-Addl. Director I&PR Department. Dt 02.02.2024

CHAPTER VII

ACCEPTANCE OF CAA FOR COMMON INTEREST

Your Grievance is registered successfully.
Registration Number: PMOPG/E/ 2024/0057208

  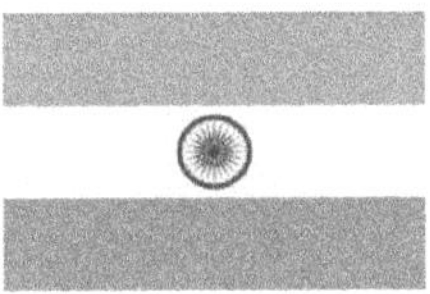

Dt. 12.03.2024

Respected Shri Narendra Modi Ji, Hon'ble Prime Minister, India

It is a much welcoming news to get acceptance of CAA in our country. However, there are opposition leaders, who cause provocations and agitate the common people. They convey the wrong and adverse remarks over such justified rules, which creates wrong and misleading impression over common mass, resulting in strike, crime, and terrorism. In view of such misleading and wrong propaganda against any rule/policy, by any person that causes provocation, the person should be punished under the court of law. Simultaneously, such wrong concepts can be challenged against the concerned parties with the election commissioner, who can take strong steps against the misinformation. This would check against falsehood and spread of misleading information among the common mass.

With heartiest regards,

Yours sincerely,

Dr. Nanda Nandan Das, Original Thinker,

ACCEPTANCE OF CAA FOR COMMON INTEREST

Chairman, People's Welfare Suggestion Forum
Dt. 12.03.2024

NARENDRA MODI,

PRIME MINISTER OF INDIA.

Grievance Concerns to
Name Of Complainant-NANDA NANDAN DAS
Date of Receipt-12/03/2024
Received By Ministry/Department-Prime Minister's Office
Grievance Description
Current Status-Case closed
Date of Action-26/03/2024
Remarks-Your suggestions are always welcome. Should you have any other suggestions Register on MyGov App. You can Follow MyGov on Twitter/Subscribe to MyGov YouTube Channel also.
Regards, CPIO MyGov
Rating-Excellent
Remarks-Satisfied

Officer Name-Office of CEO MyGov (Office of CEO MyGov)
 Organisation name-My Gov.
Contact Address-Electronics Niketan CGO Complex, New Delhi
Email Address-ceo@mygov.in
Contact Number-01124364706

CHAPTER VIII

THE CONCEPT - ALL BELONG TO THE MOTHER EARTH AND LIVE WELL

Dt. 23.11.2023

To

The Hon'ble President, G-20

(Through Special Secretary, G 20)

Sub- Peace globally.

Respected Sir,

The slogan, one Earth, One Family, and One Future, is definitely a means to achieve peace. To streamline such principles, morality, unity, and nationality are essential among all. Therefore, the moral value in the educational system, in the concept of all belonging to Mother Earth, stay here for a certain time. The concept of religions, castes, and border lines of countries were framed after human beings, turned from wild to social in the course of time. So, all human beings are the same, and nothing belongs to anyone. Only good humanity among all can bring peace. All countries should ensure terrorism-free activity. A sample course on moral science is attached herewith for ready reference, to be followed by all to streamline morality, unity, and nationality. Due to such principles, the war, like that of Israel-Hamas, Russia-Ukraine, etc. would be differed, and crime and terrorism would be minimized.

With heartiest regards,

Yours sincerely,

Dr. Nanda Nandan Das, Original Thinker

Chairman, People's Welfare Suggestion Forum.

Dt. 23.11.2023

NARENDRA MODI, PRIME MINISTER OF INDIA.

CHAPTER IX

GOLD RESERVE- SUPPORT FINANCIAL STABILITY

Your Grievance is registered successfully.
Registration Number: PMOPG/E/2024/0074150

Date: 19th April 2024
Respected Shri Narendra Modi Ji, Hon'ble Prime Minister of India,

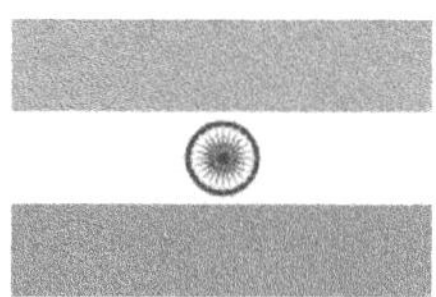

I believe that the 'Gold Reserve' in our country plays a crucial role in supporting its financial stability. I am aware that significant efforts are being made to increase the gold reserves in the country. In this regard, I would like to draw your attention to a suggestion, I have submitted with registration number: PMOPG/E/2019/0507844, regarding the concept of 'Gold Backing of a Country.'

I believe that implementing this suggestion could provide additional financial support to our nation, if deemed appropriate.
With warm regards,
Yours sincerely,
Dr. Nanda Nandan Das, Original Thinker
Former Secretary, Works Government of Odisha
Chairman, People's Welfare Suggestion Forum
Date: 19th April 2024
Name Of Complainant-NANDA NANDAN DAS
Date of Receipt-19/04/2024
NARENDRA MODI,
PRIME MINISTER OF INDIA

CHAPTER X

WEBINAR ON HEALTH CARE- 'HEALTH IS WEALTH'

Registration Number: PMOPG/E/2024/0037383   Dt. 17.02.2024

Respected Shri Narendra Modi Ji, Hon'ble Prime Minister, India

It is regarding health care of all the students and common mass of the country. The summary of the 96th webinar of Thinkers' Club, followed herewith, may please be referred, which is self – explanatory.   With heartiest regards,

Yours faithfully,

Dr. Nanda Nandan Das, Original Thinker,

Former Secretary, Works Govt. of Odisha,

Chairman, People's Welfare Suggestion Forum

Dt. 17.02.2024

THINKERS' CLUB

Cuttack-753001, (M) 9861145687

12th February 2024.

Topic- Discussion on Importance of Health is Wealth.

About 18 million people die in world every year due to heart related ailments. Our country is elevated to the diabetes capital of the world.

The 96th webinar of Thinkers' Club, was held on 11-2-2024, presided by Shri Barada Prasanna Das, President of the Club. The focus of the discussion was on 'health is wealth', its preventive measures and generating such awareness among common people.

Sri Ranjan Biswal, Advisor, Niramaya Govt. of Odisha, Dr Jayanta Panda, Professor and Head of the Department Medicine, SCB Medical College, Dr Sur Kishore Mishra, Head of the Cardiac Department, SCB Medical College and Mrs Swapna Rani Patra, an advisor to the SCB Medical College were experts to discuss on different aspects of human health. They were of the opinion that the people at present going sick due to their life style, stress at workplace, food habits, and environmental factors. The common diseases that are rampant are diabetes, high blood pressure, cardiac problems, obesity, insomnia, and cancer. They suggested that people of all ages:

- To do exercise for at least 30 minutes a day, 5 days in a week. Avoidance of exercises creates problems in all sectors of life.
- The people should sleep for 6 to 7 hours per day.
- Maintain their body weight, referring to vital tables.
- Avoid consuming junk foods and processed foods.
- They should make a habit of consuming fruits and fibrous foods.
- The fruits and vegetables which are off-season are not healthy.
- One should avoid smoking and consuming alcohol. Those who are not in the habit, shouldn't start it, and those who are already in the habit should give up.
- The doctors advised citizens to obtain a copy of the book, "Calories Content of Indian Foods" prepared by the National Institute of Nutrition, Hyderabad. This book describes the food value of different Indian foods, and this can be taken as a reference to all categories of foods and patients.

Dr. Nanda Nandan Das, Original Thinker, expressed the point wise preventive measures for care of health, should be communicated to Hon'ble Prime Minister, India, which can be inculcated in educational system, so that there would be awareness on health care among the students and common citizens. It is also requested to include the valued further suggestions on the health care of other Allopathic, Naturopathy, and Ayurveda experts of the nation.

The meeting was attended by

Dr Nanda Nandan Das, Binod Mohanty, Dr Manoj Mahapatra from Jamshedpur, Kalipada Tripathy from Japan, Subash Sahoo from Baharin, Shuvendu Panda from Indonesia, Pratap Rout from Chhatish Garha, Prof Pramod Satapathy, Chitaranjan Satapathy from Delhi, Prof Purnima Mitra, Dr Amulya Choudhury, Prof

Jayakrushna Choudhury, Bibhudutta Mohanty from Bangalore and many more in the U.Tube.

The members participated, made a request to send a memorandum to the honorable Prime Minister of India, describing the present plight of the common people in the state and country, suggesting some remedial measures.

Dr Nanda Nandan Das, Original Thinker, took the responsibility of sending this memorandum.

Barada Prasanna Das

President, Thinkers' Club

12.02.2024

Name Of Complainant-NANDA NANDAN DAS

Date of Receipt-17/02/2024

Received By Ministry/Department-Prime Minister's Office

Grievance Description

Current Status-Case closed

Date of Action-29/04/2024

Remarks--Thank You. Your suggestions are always welcome.

Should you have any other suggestions Register on MyGov App.

You can Follow MyGov on Twitter/Subscribe to MyGov YouTube Channel also. Regards, CPIO MyGov

Office of CEO MyGov (Office of CEO MyGov)

Organisation name-My Gov.

Contact Address: -Electronics Niketan CGO Complex, New Delhi

Email Address-ceo@mygov.in

Contact Number-01124364706

CHAPTER XI

OPTIMIZING USE OF LAXMI BUS IN ODISHA TO MINIMIZE THE LOSSES

NANDA NANDAN DAS
From: nandanandan_das@yahoo.com
To: adc.odishagovernor@gmail.com, CMO ODISHA
Cc: Nandanandan Das
Fri, Aug 23 at 10:12 AM
NANDANANDAN DAS
From: nandanandan_das@yahoo.com
To: Dharmendra Pradhan, av.odisha@sansad.nic.in
Cc: Nandanandan Das
Fri, Aug 23 at 10:24 AM
For Favor of kind information Sir,
Dr. Nanda Nandan Das, Original Thinker
Ph-9437617604
Dt.23.08.2024

Dt. 23.08.2024
To
The Hon'ble Governor of Odisha
The Hon'ble Chief Minister of Odisha
Subject: Addressing Financial Losses and Optimizing Use of Laxmi Buses
Respected Sir,
I hope this letter finds you well. It has come to my attention that the Laxmi Buses, which were established to enhance passenger transportation, are currently facing a substantial financial loss exceeding ₹300 crores. There should be accountability for creation of such liability. These buses are reportedly running with very few passengers, leading to significant financial strain.

Given the current situation, it is imperative that we explore alternative solutions to maximize the utility of these assets. It has been mentioned by a spokesperson of BJD that these buses were introduced to provide subsidized transportation to citizens in remote areas. While the intent was commendable, the execution seems to have led to unforeseen challenges.

In light of this, I respectfully request that consideration be given to deploying smaller buses or larger four-wheel vehicles with a capacity of 10-15 passengers for the transportation needs of people in remote areas. This adjustment could help mitigate the financial losses while still fulfilling the goal of providing accessible transportation.

Thank you for your attention to this matter. I look forward to your positive response and the steps that will be taken to address these issues.

Yours sincerely,

Dr. Nanda Nandan Das, Original Thinker
Former Secretary, Works, Government of Odisha
Former Chairman, OB&CC
Chairman, People's Welfare Suggestion Forum
Ex-Chairman, Odisha Durneeti Sangharsa Mancha
Phone: 9437617604
Dt. 23.08.2024

CHAPTER XII

OVERCOMING THE ACUTE SHORTAGE OF DOCTORS IN ODISHA

Mon, Aug 26 at 12:40 PM

Dea Sir,

The proposal to overcome the Acute Shortage of Doctors in Odisha is forwarded for favour of your kind information.

With regards,
Yours sincerely,
Dr. Nanda Nandan Das, Original Thinker
Former Secretary, Works, Government of Odisha
Chairman, People's Welfare Suggestion Forum
Date: 26.08.2024
From: nandanandan_das@yahoo.com
To: adc.odishagovernor@gmail.com, CMO ODISHA
Cc: Nandanandan Das, Barada Prasanna Das
Mon, Aug 26 at 12:32 PM
26.08.2024
To
The Hon'ble Governor, Odisha
The Hon'ble Chief Minister, Odisha
Subject: Proposal to Overcome the Acute Shortage of Doctors
Respected Sir,
I am writing to draw your attention to a pressing issue regarding the acute shortage of doctors in government service. In an effort to address this concern, I had previously submitted a suggestion to the Hon'ble Chief Minister, Odisha, as detailed in Letter No. 276 dated 20.06.2016 of the People's Welfare Suggestion Forum

(PWSF). However, as there has been no response from the government, I also forwarded the same proposal to the Hon'ble Prime Minister of India, as per Registration Number PMOPG/E/2019/0621282 Dt.19.10.2019.

For your reference and review, I have enclosed a copy of the aforementioned letter. I kindly request that you consider this proposal and take appropriate action if deemed suitable. Thank you for your attention to this matter.

With heartiest regards,
Yours sincerely,
Dr. Nanda Nandan Das
Original Thinker
Former Secretary, Works, Government of Odisha
Chairman, People's Welfare Suggestion Forum
Date: 26.08.2024
Enclosure: Copy of previous letter

PEOPLE'S WELFARE SUGGESTION FORUM
COUNTRY FIRST

REGD. NO: 1567/2008 (TRUST)
OFFICE PLOT NO - 2024, CHINTAMANISWAR AREA,
BHUBANESWAR, PIN-751006, ODISHA
Ph- 09437617604, E-Mail- nandanandan_das@yahoo.com

L. No. 276,   dt. 20.06.2016
To
The Chief Minister, Odisha
Sub-Proposal to overcome the acute shortage of doctors.
Sir,

This forum (PWSF) is an apolitical organization (Acting as THINK TANK) of senior citizens and younger professionals from various disciplines including education, engineering, forestry, finance, land revenue and other disciplines which provides suggestions to government on burning issues facing the country.

There is acute shortage of doctors in Odisha like most parts of India. For this, the retirement age of doctors has been increased to 65 years at the national level. No doubt, it is a good decision. Though it may ease the situation to some extent, it is not a permanent solution and will not meet the entire shortage.

OVERCOMING THE SHORTAGE OF DOCTORS IN ODISHA

The reason of scarcity of doctors for government service is mainly due to heavy expenditure incurred for admission and study in private medical colleges, though it is much less in the government colleges. The young doctors after passing out from the colleges, like to serve in private hospitals, nursing homes and clinics in larger cities or take up private practice with lucrative earnings rather than joining   government service to be posted to rural areas, with difficult working conditions and limited earning. At the same time very good scholars, interested in pursuing medical line are deprived due to financial hardship.

It is suggested to reserve the requisite seats in all government medical colleges for the students who are interested to serve in government service for minimum period of 30 years, out of which 15 years should be spent in rural service with proper agreement. The entire expenditure for the study will be borne by the government. The ratio of medical students, i.e., 1. For government service and 2. Other doctors, can be decided yearly for meeting the demand of government doctors in future. By this, the meritorious students, debar of studying medical science due to financial crisis, can get chance to become doctors. The selection of government doctors should be based on merit only in order to maintain transparency. In such case the retirement age of doctors can continue to be at par with other services of government.

If selections of medical students have been already made then option to switch over to government special quota can be taken from the students and the entire course fee can be borne by government in such cases, after due signing of agreement. In case of violation, the erring doctor should be liable to forfeit his/her MCI registration.

This may be considered by the government in order to overcome the situation arising due to shortage of doctors.

Yours faithfully,

Dt-20.06.2016

Dr Nanda Nandan Das

Chairman, People's Welfare Suggestion Forum

Copy to Hon'ble Minister, Health, Chief Secretary, Development Commissioner, Secretary, Health for favour of information and necessary action.

Dr. Nanda Nandan Das

CHAPTER XIII

MAINTAINING DISCIPLINE IN PARLIAMENT AND ASSEMBLY

Grievance Registration Number: PMOPG/E/2024/0106730

Dt. 03.07.2024

Respected Shri Narendra Modi Ji, Hon'ble Prime Minister of India, it has come to our attention that during Thanks Giving Ceremony for the Hon'ble President of India in the Parliament on dt. 02.07.2024, some MPs from opposition parties disrupted the speech of Hon'ble Prime Minister, India by shouting loudly for 2 hours and 17 minutes. This behaviour is not in line with the expectations of the electorate, who entrust their MPs with the responsibility of addressing the nation's welfare.

Unfortunately, despite over seven decades of independence, some voters continue to cast their votes based on a give-and-take basis, leading to the election of indiscipline MPs. This was exemplified in yesterday proceedings. The Parliament is a sacred place where critical issues and national policies are deliberated and decided. Continuous disturbances hinder productive debate and, ultimately, the country's progress.

MPs are remunerated from public funds, including their salaries and pensions. Therefore, the disruptive actions witnessed on 02.07.2024 should not be tolerated. It is imperative to take proper action against MPs and MLAs who cause disturbances by shouting and sloganeering in Parliament and Assembly sessions here after. Ensuring decorum in these legislative bodies will create a conducive environment for meaningful discussions and decisions on issues and policies critical to our nation's progress.

Yours sincerely,

Dr. Nanda Nandan Das, Original Thinker

Chairman, People's Welfare Suggestion Forum

Er. Ambika Ballabha Swain, Addl. Secretary, PWSF

Dt. 03.07.2024

CHAPTER XIV

PM'S VISIT TO UKRAINE – A SYMBOL OF PEACE

NANDANANDAN DAS
From: nandanandan_das@yahoo.com
To: Dharmendra Pradhan, av.odisha@sansad.nic.in
Cc: Nandanandan Das
Sun, Aug 25 at 7:35 PM
This is concerned to the state of Odisha and submitted for kind information Sir.
Dr. Nanda Nandan Das, Original thinker. Dt.25.08.2024

NANDANANDAN DAS
From: nandanandan_das@yahoo.com
To: adc.odishagovernor@gmail.com, CMO ODISHA
Cc: Nandanandan Das
Sun, Aug 25 at 7:22 PM NANDANANDAN DAS

Dt. 25.08.2024

To
The Hon'ble Governor of Odisha,
The Hon'ble Chief Minister of Odisha

Subject: (A) Why I stand for suggesting to Hon'ble PM and Heads of Odisha Government And (B) PM's Visit to Ukraine and Russia – A Symbol of Peace Respected Sir,

I hope, this letter finds you in good health and high spirit.

    (A) Why I stand for suggesting to Hon'ble PM and Heads of Odisha Government
Sir, I am an Original Thinker i.e. I never borrow, hire or quote the examples of any saints or great persons, not even quote anything

from ethics on any of my script. I am very much updated in current affairs visualizing news. The solutions to national, international critical issues appear to me, without earlier notice, even in odd hours instantaneously. Such performances have been continuing since after joining in my service. As an engineer, my concepts were all the times appreciated by my higher authorities being innovative original ones. After I became E.I.C. and Secretary, my innovative methods were used for construction of stable roads, control of road accidents, strong long-lasting buildings, disaster management and maintaining transparency in distribution of LC and circulated to different departments as ideal guidelines. There is no practical based book for civil engineers, so Dr. Sanjay Patro, Head of the Department, Civil of VSSUT and Dr. Aditya Das, NIT, Rourkela prepared a practical based book FINE TUNING OF ROAD AND BUILDING PROJECT, me as the author, available on Amazon.

I am of age 80+ and have been retired for 22 years. Since then, I keep myself engaged in social work. I am also restlessly going on suggesting innovative concepts on introduction of Moral Science as compulsory subject; Poverty free Odisha; Control of Overdraft; Land Reform, Compulsory Marriage Registration; Solving Chit Fund Issue; Control of Flood; Control of Road Accidents; Green Odisha; Wild Life Preservation and many more suggestions but there was no response from the previous government. My suggestion on control of Overdraft was strictly followed after apprising on the matter to Shri Prafulla Ghadei, the then Minister of Finance during March 2005, the Overdraft got controlled fully in 2006. If my suggestions would have been properly scrutinized and followed in our state, in the successive years too, I can confidently say, the state would have been poverty free developed state, by now.

I was very much encouraged by Shri Narendra Modi Ji, Hon'ble Prime Minister during 2019, after getting his message 'Welcome Nandanandan- Now you'll be the first to

- Get daily updates and messages from the P.M.
- Write directly to the P.M. Share your thoughts on any issue or policy.

PM'S VISIT TO UKRAINE- A SYMBOL OF PEACE

Since then, I am going on suggesting solutions to various issues, which have been subsequently made into 10 books of 'LETTERS TO THE HON'BLE PRIME MINISTER', available on Amazon.

I have sent my book Global Peace to heads of 170 countries during November 2017. There was a meet on Global Peace between President of North Korea and President of America at Singapore on 12. 06.2018. I am happy that the two heads of states received my book 'Global Peace'.

I belong to the state of Odisha. I have tried every time, to improve financial status of the state, a poverty free developed Odisha. So, I have tried to propose many innovative practical based suggestions to the government of Odisha but all my proposals were ignored. Due to my personal appraisal with Shri Prafulla Ghadei, the then Finance Minister, there could be control of Overdraft, for which at least the government servants are getting their salary monthly till date.

Being a native of State of Odisha, some of the proposals, suggested to the Hon'ble PM, pertaining to national and international issues, though not concerned to our state, are intimated to your-kind-self for favour of information.

(B)The proposal, already sent to the Hon'ble Prime Minister, India is presented herewith in favour of your kind information.

PM's Visit to Ukraine and Russia – A Symbol of Peace
Your Grievance is registered successfully.
Registration Number: PMOPG/E/2024/0130986

Dt.24.08.2024
PM's Visit to Ukraine and Russia – A Symbol of Peace

Respected Narendra Modi Ji, Hon'ble Prime Minister of India,
1.   Your visit to Russia and recent visit to Ukraine on August 23, 2024, symbolizes not only a step toward halting the conflict between these nations but also a message for global peace. Your positive relationships with the leaders of both countries are encouraging and fostering hope for reconciliation.

I respectfully suggest that you consider inviting both leaders to India for a peace conference in the near future. Such a meeting could be pivotal in promoting peace and addressing global terrorism.

2. The initial terrorist attack by Hamas on Israel resulted in loss of lives, property damage, and severe distress. In response, Israel took measures against Hamas, including targeting terrorist infrastructure. Some Islamic countries, rather than condemning terrorism, chose to support Hamas due to shared religious affiliations. This has led to further violence and destruction, as seen in recent attacks on Hindus and others in Bangladesh. Some nations, by fostering terrorism and crime, contribute to widespread unrest and poverty.

3.   Human civilization, from its beginnings in Mesopotamia, spread all over the world and has developed languages, religions, and borders. However, some leaders, driven by ego and a desire for expansion, create conflict that affects all of humanity. Ultimately, we all share the same planet and are bound by the same fate. Discussions at peace conferences should address the need for unity and the cessation of war-mongering and terrorism. Such discussions could alleviate global suffering and promote peace.

With warm regards,

Dr. Nanda Nandan Das, Original Thinker

Former Secretary, Works, Government of Odisha

Chairman, People's Welfare Suggestion Forum

August 24, 2024.

This is for favour of information. With warm regards,

Yours Sincerely,

Dr. Nanda Nandan Das, Original Thinker

Former Secretary, Works, Government of Odisha

Dt.25.08.2024

Phone: 9437617604

CHAPTER XV

UKRAINE TRIP OF PRIME MINISTER – THE QUEST FOR GLOBAL PEACE

Grievance is registered successfully
Registration Number: PMOPG/E/2024/0107741

Dt. 05.07.2024

Respected Shri Narendra Modi Ji, Hon'ble Prime Minister of India,

The war between Russia and Ukraine has been ongoing for more than two years. This conflict is not only a man-made disaster for both the countries involved but also for the entire world. As it is understood, Ukraine's desire to join NATO and Russia's opposition to it have become the root cause of this war. This vindictive attitude from both sides has mostly ruined Ukraine and inflicted great losses on Russia, affecting all countries globally.

As you are scheduled to visit Russia soon, in the interest of achieving global peace, I humbly request you to appeal to the Hon'ble President of Russia to cease hostilities and consider the broader implications for humanity. Simultaneously, it is essential that the Hon'ble President of Ukraine also seeks to end the conflict through mutual understanding. Continuing this war benefits no one, especially when approximately one-third of Ukraine has already been affected, resulting in significant loss of property and lives.

Universal truth is that all mankind belongs to the Earth like other living beings and the temporary nature of our existence on Earth. Nothing belongs to anybody. To maintain peace, verdicts of United Nation dt. 24.10.1945 i.e. international laws established to maintain global peace and security should be yard stick for all countries.

Some nations are encouraging President Zelenskyy to maintain a war stance, which is detrimental to any country's well-being. Therefore, President Zelenskyy should reconsider not joining NATO. Both the countries should aim to build friendly relations and mutual understanding to ensure peace in their own lands and contribute to global peace.

With heartiest regards,

Yours sincerely,

Dr. Nanda Nandan Das, Original Thinker

Former Secretary, Works Govt. Of Odisha

Chairman, People's Welfare Suggestion Forum

Dt. 05.07.2024

  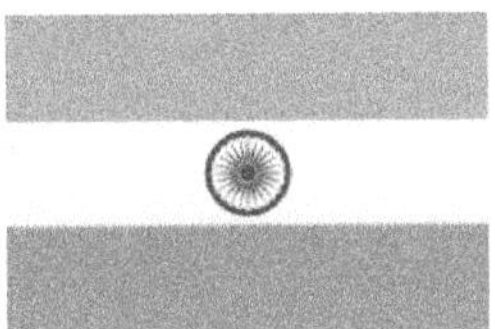

NARENDRA MODI,
Prime Minister of India

CHAPTER XVI

RENAMING THE INDIA AS HINDUSTAN/ BHARAT

Registration Number: PMOPG/E/2024/0126413

Name Of Complainant-NANDA NANDAN DAS
Date of Receipt-15/08/2024
Received By Ministry/Department-Prime Minister's Office
Grievance Description
15.08.2024
Respected Sri Narendra Modi Ji. Hon'ble Prime Minister, India,
HAPPY INDEPENDENCE DAY.
This is regarding 'Renaming India as Hindustan/Bharat'.
The details of reasons to consider for renaming Hindustan/Bharat
is put forth on the 78th independence in attached file, which is self-
explanatory. With heartiest regards,
Yours sincerely,
Dr. Nanda Nandan Das, Original Thinker
Chairman, Peoples Welfare Suggestion Forum.
Former Secretary, Works Govt. of Odisha
Former, Chairman, OB&CC
15.08.2024
Grievance Document   Current Status-Case closed
Date of Action-27/08/2024

Remarks- Your suggestions are always welcome. Should you have
any other suggestions Register on MyGov App. You can Follow
MyGov on Twitter/Subscribe to MyGov YouTube Channel also.
Regards, CPIO MyGov
Officer Name-Office of CEO MyGov (Office of CEO MyGov)
Organisation name-My Gov.
Contact Address-Electronics Niketan CGO Complex, New Delhi
Email Address-ceo@mygov.in, Contact Number-01124364706

PEOPLE'S WELFARE SUGGESTION FORUM
COUNTRY FIRST

Regd. No.: 1567 / 2008 (Trust)
Bhubaneswar: Plot- 2024, Chintamaniswar Colony,
Pin - 751006, Odisha
Bhadrak-Baudpur, Post- Madhab Nagar,
Dist. -Bhadrak, Pin-756181-Odisha
Ph.: 9437617604, 9437312986,
Email: nandanandan_das@yahoo.com

Dt. 15.08.2024   1:40am
Country First

To
Shri Narendra Modi Ji, the Hon'ble Prime Minister of India
Subject: Renaming India as Hindustan/Bharat
Respected Sir,
Wish you Happy Independence Day.
I hope this letter finds you in good health and high spirits. I am writing to you on behalf of the People's Welfare Suggestion Forum (PWSF), an apolitical think tank comprising senior citizens and young professionals from various disciplines, including education, engineering, finance, and land revenue. Our forum has previously contributed to significant national initiatives, such as the introduction of the Aadhaar Card.
We are reaching out to address a matter of profound national importance, the renaming of India as Hindustan. We believe this proposal warrants serious consideration given the current geopolitical and sociopolitical climate.

HISTORICAL CONTEXT AND CURRENT CRISIS
Historically, the land known today as India was Sanatan culture basically of Hindu-Dharma. It has witnessed the rise and fall of many civilizations and has been shaped by various religious and cultural influences. The partition of British India in 1947 led to the creation of India and Pakistan, with India envisioned as a secular nation (as majority, this would have been homeland for Hindus) and Pakistan as a homeland for Muslims. Despite the secular nature of the Indian Constitution, it is evident that the religious

demographic and its implications on national identity have been subjects of intense debate.

Recent events in neighbouring countries such as Bangladesh, Pakistan, and Afghanistan, where religious minorities (origin-native) have faced persecution, highlight a growing concern about the safety and security of religious communities. In Bangladesh, for example, the resignation of Prime Minister Sheikh Hasina has led to increased violence against Hindus, with numerous reports of destruction of religious institutions and properties.

The concerns extend beyond immediate geopolitical issues. The rise of terrorism, poverty, and sectarian violence in various parts of the world, particularly in some Islamic countries, underscores the urgency of addressing these challenges. The issue of religious intolerance and its impact on global peace and security cannot be ignored.

PROPOSAL FOR RENAMING:

There is no Hindu Country in the world. The present opposite parties have started to bias fabricated imaginary facts to the Muslims community to gain a vote bank. A MP could utter joy-Palestine during oath taking ceremony, dis-honouring nationalism. Time may come, India to face Bangladesh situation, killing and damaging property of Hindus to make them minority. The Sanatan culture always give importance to other religions and never act hostile, unless face adverse situation. In light of these challenges, we propose the consideration of renaming India as Hindustan or Bharat. This change could serve several purposes:

1.   Strengthening National Identity as Indians/Bharatiya/ Hindustani with concept of Country First: Renaming the country could reinforce its cultural and historical identity, emphasizing its heritage and the values of Sanatan Dharma.

2.   Providing Shelter and Security: By identifying more closely with its Hindu roots, India could offer a refuge for Hindus, Sikhs, Jain etc. of India-origin worldwide, who face persecution, ensuring their safety and preserving the cultural heritage.

3.   Addressing Internal and External Challenges: A clear national identity might help mitigate internal conflicts and provide a stronger stance in addressing external pressures and threats.

Concerns about Political Implications:

We are aware of the political sensitivities surrounding this issue. The proposal to rename the country must be approached with a balanced perspective, considering the diverse viewpoints of all communities within India. It is crucial that any such change is carried out with broad consensus and respect for the secular principles enshrined in the Constitution.

To bring feeling of morality, unity and nationality among all citizens, a course of moral science as a compulsory subject from class 1 to graduation was suggested to Ministry of Human resources during 2009 and to Hon'ble Prime Minister, India in Registration Number PMOPG/E/2019 /0640330 dt. 01.11.2019. Through such moral value, only ideal Indians of Outstanding, Exceptional character with morality, unity and nationality having concept of Country First, irrespective of religions, castes, and other differences, would be generated.

1.   OUTSTANDING –honest, sincere, and progressive
2.   EXCEPTIONAL- honest, sincere, progressive, and creative citizens,

CONCLUSION:

In conclusion, while the renaming of India as Hindustan/ Bharat is a significant and potentially transformative step, it must be undertaken with careful deliberation and inclusivity. We urge the government to consider this proposal in the context of safeguarding national security, fostering unity, and preserving cultural heritage.

We trust that you will give this matter the serious consideration it deserves and look forward to a constructive discussion on this important issue. With warm regards,

Yours sincerely,

Dr. Nanda Nandan Das, Original Thinker

Chairman, Peoples Welfare Suggestion Forum.

Former Secretary, Works Govt. of Odisha

Former, Chairman, OB&CC

Shri Barada Prasanna Das, Secretary, Er. Ambika Ballav Swain, Addl. Secretary,,Er. Kamala Kanta Behera, Vice Chairman, Shri Akshay Kumar Panda, Asst. Secretary, Dr. K. M. Mahapatra, Jt. Secretary.

Dt. 15.08.2024

CHAPTER XVII

CONTROL OF FLOOD SITUATION IN DELHI FOR YAMUNA OVERFLOW

Grievance is registered successfully.
Registration Number: PMOPG/E/2024/0106725
Dt. 03.07.2024
Respected Shri Narendra Modi Ji,
Hon'ble Prime Minister, India
Recently, due to the highest rainfall in Delhi in a century, the city has faced a disaster, leading to loss of lives and properties, transportation issues, water scarcity, blockage of daily domestic and official transactions, disruption of healthcare services, commercial transactions, and many more.

I have already suggested to your kind self, in registration number: PMOPG/E/2023/0137731 Dt. 11.07.2023, about the Control of Flood in Urban Areas due to Storm Water. This topic was also discussed in the 76th international webinar of the Thinkers Club on 09.07.2023. To control the flood situation in Delhi due to blocked drains and inadequate provision of designed sections of drains, the solution was proposed earlier to the Chief Minister of Delhi.

The key points cited may be scrutinized in detail, and the last rainfall data in a day, being the maximum in a century, may be considered for the design purpose. If there would be sincerity in design, execution, and regular strict maintenance by the engineers, I can assure you that the flood situation in Delhi due to storm water can be controlled.

Similarly, a proposal was sent to the Hon'ble Prime Minister in registration number: PMOPG/E/2023 /0138801 Dt. 13.07.2023 on Flood Control in Delhi for Yamuna Overflow. The proposal aims to control the flood due to the Yamuna River in Delhi. The key points cited therein should be properly scrutinized, detailed surveyed, properly designed, sincerely executed, and honestly timely maintained. This would surely become a stable permanent method to overcome such flood situations in Delhi.

The members present during discussion:

With heartiest regards,

Yours sincerely,

Dr. Nanda Nandan Das, Original Thinker

Former Secretary, Works Govt. of Odisha

Chairman, People's Welfare Suggestion Forum

Er. Ambika Ballabha Swain, Addl. Secretary, PWSF

Dt. 03.07.2024

Grievance Status for Registration Number:
PMOPG/E/2024/0106725

Name Of Complainant-NANDA NANDAN DAS

Date of Receipt-03/07/2024

Received By Ministry/Department-Prime Minister's Office

Current Status-Grievance Received

Date of Action-03/07/2024

Officer Concerns To-Forwarded to Prime Minister's Office

Officer Name-Mukul Dixit, Under Secretary (Public)

Organisation name-Prime Minister's Office

Contact Address-Public Wing 5th Floor, Rail Bhawan New Delhi

Email Address-us-public.sb@gov.in

Contact Number-011-23386447

Current Status-Case closed

Date of Action-18/07/2024

Remarks-The data of grievance number PMOPG/E/2023/0137731 is not available in the ID of GNCTD. Contents are generalized.

Rating-Poor

Rating Remarks-Not Satisfied

CONTROL OF FLOOD SITUATION IN DELHI

Officer Concerns To-Officer Name-DEPUTY SECY. PGC (Dy Secretary)
Organisation name-Government of NCT of Delhi
Contact Address-Public Grievances Commission M Block Vikas Bhawan I P Estate New Delhi
Email Address- pgcdelhi@nic.in
Contact Number-01123379900

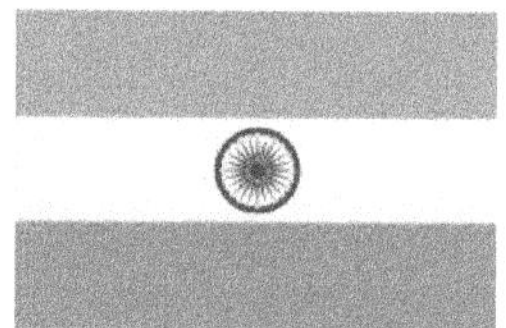

NARENDRA MODI
PRIME MINISTER INDIA

Current Status-Case closed
Date of Action-18/07/2024
Remarks
The data of grievance number PMOPG/E/2023/0137731 is not available in the ID of GNCTD. Contents are generalized.
Rating-Poor
Rating Remarks-Not Satisfied
DEPUTY SECY. PGC (Dy Secretary)
Organisation name-Government of NCT of Delhi
Contact Address-Public Grievances Commission, M Block Vikas Bhawan I P Estate New Delhi
Email Address-pgcdelhi@nic.in
Contact Number-01123379900

CHAPTER XVIII

SOLUTIONS TO HUMAN AND WILD LIFE CONFLICT

There has been a loss of lives and damage to property caused by elephants, as well as the killing of elephants by local communities. Similarly, conflicts between humans and other wild animals, such as tigers, foxes, and others, have resulted in harm to both humans and animals. Miscreants have also been involved in the killing of wildlife.

In order to address this issue, suggestions were submitted in different time periods to Shri Jairam Ramesh, the then minister of Sri Jairam Ramesh, the Hon'ble Ministry of Environment & Forests, in letter number 137 dt.14.07.2009 of PWSF, Hon'ble PM, India, vide registration Number: PMOPG/E/2019/0621457 Dt. 19.10.2019 (CHAPTER XII OF THE BOOK LETTERS TO THE HON'BLE PRIME MINISTER). Similar proposals were suggested to the Hon'ble PM of India-vide registration number PMOPG/E/2024/0133269 dated 30.08.2024, and further communicated to the Hon'ble Governor of Odisha and the Chief Minister of Odisha on 30.08.2024. Since the proposals are innovative concepts, need to be reviewed by responsible and capable authorities, possess a research-oriented mentality, rather than junior staff. This could lead to a successful resolution of the problem.

Dt: 30.08.2024

NANDANANDAN DAS
From: nandanandan_das@yahoo.com
To: CMO ODISHA
Cc: Nandanandan Das
Fri, Aug 30 at 11:36 AM
Dt. 30.08.2024

SOLUTIONS TO HUMAN AND WILDLIFE CONFLICT

To
The Hon'ble Chief Minister, Odisha
Sub- Urgent Review and Action Required on Human-Wildlife
Conflict Management
Respected Sir,
I have suggested the proposal to solve Human-Wildlife Conflict
Management to the Hon'ble Prime Minister, India today vide
Registration Number: PMOPG/E/2024/0133269 Dt. 30.08.2024.
The same is followed herewith, it is self-explanatory. Such matter
should be scrutinized through the experts (not at junior level) to
find the problems face by attack of elephants. A letter addressed to
you on 28.08.2024 from under signed on such matter may please
be referred to. With heartiest regards,
Yours sincerely
Dr. Nanda Nandan Das, Original Thinker
Chairman, People's Welfare Suggestion Forum
Chairman, Odisha Durneeti Sangharsa Mancha
Ph: 9437617604
Dt: 30.08.2024

THE TOPIC SUGGESTED TO THE HON'BLE PRIME
MINISTER, INDIA
Your Grievance is registered successfully.
Registration Number: PMOPG/E/2024/0133269
Urgent Review and Action Required on Human-Wildlife Conflict
Management
Dt. 30.08.2024
Respected Shri Narendra Modi Ji, Hon'ble Prime Minister of
India,
I hope this message finds you in good health and spirits.
I am writing to draw your esteemed attention to the ongoing and
escalating issue of human-wildlife conflict that has been affecting
various states across India, particularly in Odisha, Uttar Pradesh,
and other regions. Recent incidents, including the damage to
property and loss of lives caused by elephant attacks in Odisha,
and similar distressing occurrences involving foxes and tigers in
UP and other states, underscore the urgent need for a
comprehensive and innovative approach to address these conflicts.

In response to these critical issues, I had previously submitted a proposal to your office under registration number: PMOPG/E/2019/0621457 dated 19.10.2019. This proposal outlines a multi-faceted strategy designed to mitigate human-wildlife conflicts through the following key elements:

Strengthening Domicile Relations: Developing strategies to enhance coexistence between humans and wildlife.

Tourism Development: Creating sustainable tourist facilities to promote awareness and generate local income.

Local Income Generation: Initiatives to raise local income and improve community livelihoods as a means of reducing dependency on areas frequented by wildlife.

Government Revenue: Mechanisms to increase government revenue through eco-tourism and other related activities.

Given the gravity of the situation and its national significance, I kindly request that the proposal be reviewed with the utmost priority by experts in the field (beyond junior levels) to explore and implement effective solutions. I am confident that with the right focus and expert analysis, we can devise a strategy that not only addresses the immediate concerns but also contributes to long-term harmony between human communities and wildlife.

I look forward to your positive consideration of this matter and am available for any further discussions or clarifications required.

Thank you for your time and effort on this matter. With and heartiest regards,

Warm regards,
Yours sincerely
Dr. Nanda Nandan Das, Original
Thinker
Chairman, People's Welfare
Suggestion Forum
Chairman, Odisha Durneeti Sangharsa Mancha
Ph: 9437617604

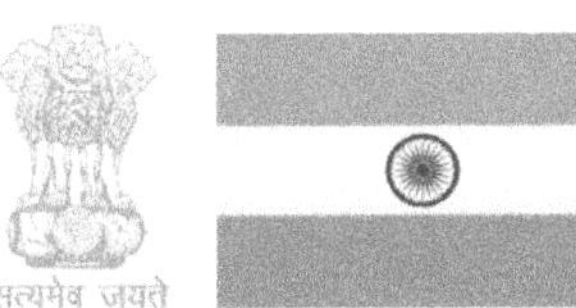

Dt: 30.08.2024

NARENDRA MODI, Prime, Minister of India

Your registration Number:
PMOPG/E/2019/0621457
Dt. 19.10.2019
Human and wild life preservation
a suggestion to hon'ble prime minister, India for human and wild life preservation.

A letter No 137 dt14.07.2009 addressed to Hon'ble Minister of Environment and Forest, India, Sub- "Human & Wildlife Preservation" is attached herewith for favour of kind consideration. The same principle can be adopted for preservation of wild life and safety of human life and property.

With regards,

Dr Nanda Nandan Das

Chairman, People's welfare Suggestion Forum.
Former Secretary, Works, Govt. of Odisha
Ph-9437617604
19.10.2019

PEOPLE'S WELFARE SUGGESTION FORUM
COUNTRY FIRST

Regd. No.: 1567 / 2008 (Trust)
Office: Plot No. 2024, Chintamaniswar Colony, Bhubaneswar-751006, Odisha, Ph.: 9437617604,
Email: nandanandan_das@yahoo.com

L.No-137   dt.14.07.2009

From Er Nanda Nandan Das, Chairman, People's Welfare Suggestion Forum

To,

Sri Jairam Ramesh
The Hon' Ministry of Environment& Forests
Paryavaram Bhavan, C.G.O Complex, Lodi Road,
New Delhi – 110003
Sub: Human & Wildlife Preservation
Respected Sir,
It is a confirmed truth that the millions of species of creatures disappeared rather vanish from our Earth, may be due to climate change. Change of environmental circumstances, natural calamities, global warming and killing of animals by human being.

The Scientists, Nationalists, Leaders, Environmentalists on the Earth have now inclined to adopt some principles of protection of the animals because they are equally important for sustaining the ecology in addition to the principle of co-existence on the Earth. Basing on the suggestions of forest and environmental experts, the laws have been framed and now it is high time to honour the law and protect the animals.

These rules restricted to keep the wild animals personally in circus and using them in zoos for exhibiting them to the visitors and earn their lively hood by showing different types of games and plays of trained animals to the people e.g. elephants, rabbits, rats, bears, monkeys and snake charmers on the street.

Nobody can deny that all creatures in the Earth are born free. All should be allowed to enjoy the freedom but the freedom to the wild animal will destroy the other living creatures including human being, if their movement of freedom is not restricted by providing them adequate space and proper corridors to live freely. Adequate green field and water for their food should be provided and at the same time restrict them not to cross the boundary of the space provided to them. Otherwise, they will create havoc in living places of human being in villages, towns, parks, streets etc. The rules framed should be strictly followed so that the animals are not killed at the sweet pleasure of the hunters. It has become very difficult to control unauthorized deforestation and hunting illegally. Therefore, due to shortage food the numbers of animals will decrease in the forest. By any means the loss of human life and the crop by the animals is also not desirable. These are only human harassment and National loss. The rules should not be one sided, it must be framed considering all the sides.

Generally, weightage to animal life is given more than human life. While preparing the law for animals, the life of human beings and National loss like damage to crops should not be ignored. People's Welfare Suggestion Forum suggests some measures to protect human lives and crops, while increasing the numbers of wild animals providing them sufficient food and health care. In the above context, the following points are suggested below for favour of consideration.

SUGGESTIONS

1. Specific area should be demarked with adequate space, green field for food corridor for free movement, water to drink for healthy livings in forest. Proper trench should be excavated all around and other suitable protection measures may be made, so that they can't come out of the notify area, damage the crops and human lives in inhabitancies around the area.

2. In our country some group of people maintain their lively hood by training the animals and playing road shows of monkeys, rats, bears, elephants, snakes etc. hereditarily. These are enjoyed by all category of people. The owners of the animals take care of the health and food for them. These families should not suffer due to one sided rule. Therefore, these persons should be allowed to keep these animals with permission of concerned forest department and they should take care of these animals and report the authorities periodically. Any increase in number, shortage and death of

animals should be reported in time to the concerned authorities. The authorities should be satisfied on the report otherwise action may be taken over the defaulters. By this principle the numbers of animals will increase. At the same time, the animals get food and proper health care.

We can site one example of taming of bear by Ramu Singh. The baby bear was about to die in the forest and Ramu saved and tamed the animal in a greater interest and the bear became domestic animal, which was moving on the road and even on the cycle freely. This animal was properly fed and medically treated whenever required and one of the disciplined family members. But on this issue Ramu Singh was sent to jail and bear was sent to the zoo for deviating the law. In such cases the law should be relaxed considering the circumstances and the intention.

3. With due permission of forest department, the animals may be allowed to be kept privately in zoo, parks, circus and in any religious places etc. so that the public can enjoy the play of trained animals. In a circus the human beings are trained, show play for enjoyment of the people for which they have to undergo tough and hard exercise and are fed to maintain their lives. Similarly, these animals can be permitted to show games in circus. The permitting authority should ensure that proper care has been taken for healthy living of animals, allowed to be kept with them.

4. The space demarked for free living of animals should specify their numbers if their growth will increase. The excess should be transferred to other places for free healthy living or even the excess animals can be exported, if required. This may be considered commercially.

5. The animals so allowed should be treated as domestic animals so that better care and better food can be arranged for them. These are the means to increasing the growth of animals, providing them food and taking proper care of health.

6. Generally, the animals kept in zoos are increasing and animals such as Siberian tigers, Asian tigers are decreasing because they are unable to live freely and deprive of the adequate food and health care. In such cases immediate necessary arrangements should be made to take care of these animals.

7. By adopting such methods, the total numbers of animals, category wise and in different area wise can be maintained. Any excess or shortage in numbers can be accounted for the forest department.

This is for favour of information and necessary consideration. It shall be a great favour, if the action taken on the matter shall be intimated to under sign. With regards,

Yours faithfully,

Nanda Nandan Das

Chairman, People's Welfare Suggestion Forum

Copy to Secretary, Environment & Forest, Additional D.G, Wild life, Ministry of Environment & Forest for favour of information and necessary action.

Sd-dt 14.07.2009

Nanda Nandan Das

Chairman, People's Welfare Suggestion Forum

NB-Extra points-In Thailand, elephant massages the human body, lion and tiger play with the people and in Singapore, Australia, America and many other developed countries, play dolphin and other animals, who are trained. Such type of scopes should be developed to facilitate the tourism, which will also encourage to increase the number of wild animals with proper health and food care.

Dr Nanda Nandan Das

CHAPTER XIX

FACILITATING SAFE ELECTION: TO AVOID HEAT STROKE

Your Grievance is registered successfully
Registration Number: PMOPG/E/2024/0098720
CONDUCTING ELECTION DURING OCTOBER, NOVEMBER AND DECEMBER TO AVOID HEAT STROKE
Dt. 17.06.2024
Respected Shree Narendra Modi Ji, Hon'ble Prime Minister India
The parliamentary with the assembly election of the country and in some states ended on 01.06.2024. The details of electoral reforms as suggested by Dr. Nanda Nandan Das to Shree Narendra Modi Ji, Hon'ble Prime Minister India in registration number PMOPG/E/2019/0643201-Dt. 03.11.2-19 may be considered for the benefit of the citizens and the country on the whole. In fact, the citizens of the country are real owners of the nation. Their convenience and mode of casting the vote to suitable leader is also a part of electoral reform. Of course, during the last election, much care was taken for senior citizens, ladies, and in total system, but it requires to be more organized.

During the last election, as it happened during hot summer, there were massive deaths and casualties due to sunstroke in the country. There are also examples of death and serious casualties of voters, poling officers, and securities in election duty due to sun stroke. Mostly, though the month of February and March are suitable for conducting election in order to avoid seasonal heat, but since these periods are the time of educational examination in different levels, may be avoided for conducting election.

As such, Dr. Das, suggested to consider conducting such general elections during the months of October, November and December, which may be suitable for all. During October-November, the area North of 23½* latitude (Tropic of cancer) and November-December the area South of 23½* latitude may be convenient for fixing time of casting vote to avoid havoc of sun-stroke. Of course, it may be deviated as per the border of the states.

A discussion on the topic was held in office of "People's Welfare Suggestion Forum' at Baudpur, Bhadrak, Odisha. The dignitaries present during the discussion cited below. Such proposal was enormously accepted and recommended to refer it to the Hon'ble Prime Minister, India, for consideration through Dr. Das in direct interaction to Hon'ble Prime Minister, India,

With heartiest regards,
Yours sincerely,
Dr. Nanda Nandan Das, Original Thinker,
Dt. 17.06.2024
Members present: Dr. Nanda Nandan Das, Ambika V Swain, Basanta Kumar Panigrahi, Umakanta Jena, Santosh Naik, Akshaya Panda, Rabi Narayan Prusti and Krushna Mohan Mahapatra.
Current Status-Case closed
Date of Action-27/06/2024
Received By Ministry/Department-Prime Minister's Office
Remarks: Your suggestions are always welcome. Should you have any other suggestions Register on MyGov App. Channel also.
Regards,
CPIO My Gov

Officer Name-Office of CEO MyGov (Office of CEO MyGov)

CHAPTER XX

BAN OF COMMUNAL PARTIES

Your Grievance is registered successfully.
Registration Number: PMOPG/E/2024/0104973
Dt. 30.06.2024
Respected Shri Narendra Modi Ji, Hon'ble Prime Minister, India
Subject: Ban on Communal and Caste-Based Political Parties
I hope this message finds you in good health and spirits. I write to bring to your esteemed attention a matter of considerable importance for the progress and unity of our nation.
It has come to notice that certain political parties, which base their ideologies on religion, caste, and regionalism, tend to prioritize their self-interests over the greater good of the nation. Such activities often create divisions among citizens and hinder the nation's progress. A recent incident highlights this issue: during an oath-taking ceremony, an MP from the AIMIM party chose to utter "Jay Palestine (Philistine)" instead of "Jay Hind," which is unparliamentarily and reflects a lack of nationalistic spirit.
Additionally, the current reservation system for SC, ST, and other backward classes etc., although well-intended, has been exploited by the creamy layer within these categories. This has resulted in continued financial suffering for many underprivileged individuals. It is proposed that these reservations should be allocated to BPL (Below Poverty Line) categories, ensuring that the benefits reach those genuinely in need. Unfortunately, political parties often avoid addressing this issue due to fear of losing votes from influential segments of these communities. We would prefer to have facilities for economically back ward category, which would be suitable for all. By this action there would be commonly feeling of nationalism irrespective all difference,
In light of these observations, it is urged that the formation of political parties based on communal, caste, and regional distinctions should be prohibited. Only those parties dedicated to the welfare of all citizens, irrespective of their backgrounds, should be permitted. Unnecessarily raising the number of political parties nationally and state wise should be minimized.

BAN OF COMMUNAL PARTIES

This proposal was discussed and unanimously accepted on 30.06.2024 during a meeting at the office of the People's Welfare Suggestion Forum (PWSF) in Bhadrak.

The following members were present and supported the proposal: [List of members]: Dr. Nanda Nandan Das, Purnima Mitra, Shree Nandan Das, Dr. Sachi Nandan Das, Ambika Balav Swain, Bijay Kumar Sahu, Kamalakanta Behera, Gayadhar Panda, Loknath Panda, Kamal ku. sil, Arup Chand, Goutam Das, Anant Narayan Panda, Abhijit Nayak, Kishor ku Sil, Rabinarayan Prusty, Akhay Panda, Prasant Ku Sahu, DR. Krushna Mohan Mohapatra.

Yours sincerely,

Dr. Nanda Nandan Das, Original Thinker,

Former Secretary, Works, Govt. of Odisha

Chairman, People's Welfare Suggestion Forum

Officer Concerns To-Forwarded to-Prime Minister's Office

Officer Name-Mukul Dixit, Under Secretary (Public)

Organisation name-Prime Minister's Office

Contact Address-Public Wing 5th Floor, Rail Bhawan New Delhi

Email Address-us-public.sb@gov.in

Contact Number-011-23386447

Current Status-Case closed

Date of Action-11/07/2024

Remarks -Your suggestions are always welcome. Should you have any other suggestions Register on MyGov App. You can Follow MyGov on Twitter/Subscribe to MyGov YouTube Channel also. Regards, CPIO MyGov

Officer Name-Office of CEO MyGov (Office of CEO MyGov)

Contact Address

Electronics Niketan CGO Complex, New Delhi

Email Address

ceo@mygov.in

Contact Number

01124364706

CHAPTER XXI

A CLARIFICATION FROM PMO

Your Grievance is registered successfully.
Registration Number: PMOPG/E/2024/0124827

Dt. 11.08.2024
REQUEST FOR KIND KNOWLEDGE OF HON'BLE PM, SHRI
NARENDRA MODI, JI
Respected Shi Narendra Modi Ji, Hon'ble Prime Minister, India
During 2019, I was encouraged to get message from Hon'ble
Prime Minister, India as follow:
Welcome Nandanandan
Now you'll be the first to:
- Get daily updates and messages from the PM.
- Write directly to the PM-share your thoughts on any issue or policy.
- Tune in to PM's Mann ki Baat' Live and gain access to show's entire playlist.
- Get access to all interviews and speeches of the PM.
- Get started now.

The message of Hon'ble Prime Minister, India to Nandanandan
sharing his thought (innovative) is mentioned in attached file.
Annexure 1
An online link to me from PM' side was created. According, I
started suggesting the solutions to different critical issues and
policies of the country to Shri Narendra Modi Ji, Hon'ble Prime
Minister, for his personal perusal and action. These have been
made nine books 'Letters to the Hon'ble Prime Minister'- (Part-
IA, IB, IC, II, III, IV, V, VI, VII). These books are available
through 'Notion Press' and Amazon. I am sure, if any developing
or under-developed country if follow them scrupulously, would be
developed.
Such initiation was made from the PM since 2019. So, whatever I
was suggesting, was properly responded by you sir. The then
officers concerned were very much well aware of this matter. I felt

happy when heard the speech of Hon'ble Prime Minister, India in UNGA that citizens of my country need reformation of UNO, whereas my write up on Reformation of UNO was sent some months earlier the PM.

Similarly, I felt very much happy to get many of my innovative concepts, such as 3 D method etc. many more are uttered by Hon'ble PM in Parliament and in open meetings.

I never suggest any grievance to PMO. Probably the then staffs have been transferred or retired, because I feel my innovative thoughts are not reaching direct to the Hon'ble PM, some examples are cited herewith.

On 05/07/2024, before visit of Hon'ble PM, India to Russia, I suggested to keep in mind some points for stop of war between Russia and Ukraine for achieving peace vide Registration Number: PMOPG/E/2024/0107741 Dt. 05/07/2024. The message received from PMO office that Current Status-Case closed, Date of Action-06/07/2024, Remarks-GEN. COMMENTS NOT CONTAINING SPECIFIC GRIEVANCE. The details are attached for kind reference of Hon'ble Prime Minister, India- Annexure 2.

This proved, out of lots of solutions for global peace, my submission would have been a micro thought on peace, which could not reach you, this might have some addition.

• My suggestion for control of flood in Delhi either for Yamuna River, or rain fed storm water acknowledged in Registration Number: PMOPG/E/2024/0106725   Dt. 03.07.2024. It was intimated over phone as follow:

Current Status-Case closed

Date of Action-18/07/2024

Remarks-The data of grievance number PMOPG/E/2023/0137731 is not available in the ID of GNCTD. Contents are generalized.

Rating-Poor

Rating Remarks-Not Satisfied

Officer Concerns To-Officer Name-DEPUTY SECY. PGC (Dy Secretary)

It is disappointed with the remark: The data of grievance number PMOPG/E/2023/0137731 is not available. Such matter is traceable from 'View Status'. I have copied the script concerned to the registration number PMOPG/E/2023/0137731 from 'View Status'-attached herewith. Annexure 3

Sometimes remarks are received that the suggestion is 'not to concerned portal'.

So, the innovative thoughts, meant for direct perusal of Hon'ble PM is not full filled, blocking on the way. Mostly, earlier method of suggesting directly to Hon'ble PM has been changed. I may be intimated through which method my innovative thoughts processes would reach too directly.

The scripts in Annexure 2 & 3 may please be revived again and may be considered by your direct appraisal.

With heartiest regards,

Yours sincerely

Dr. Nanda Nandan Das, Original Thinker

Chairman, People's Welfare Suggestion Forum

Dt. 11.08.2024

NARENDRA MODI,

THE PRIME MINISTER OF INDIA

It is disappointed with the remark: The data of grievance number PMOPG/E/2023/0137731 is not available. Such matter is traceable from 'View Status'. I have copied the script concerned to the registration number PMOPG/E/2023/0137731 from 'View Status'-attached herewith. Annexure 3

Sometimes remarks are received that the suggestion is 'not to concerned portal'.

So, the innovative thoughts, meant for direct perusal of Hon'ble PM is not full filled, blocking on the way. Mostly, earlier method of suggesting directly to Hon'ble PM has been changed. I may be intimated through which method my innovative thoughts processes would reach to directly.

The scripts in Annexure 2 & 3 may please be revived again and may be considered by your direct appraisal.

With heartiest regards,

Yours sincerely

Dr. Nanda Nandan Das, Original Thinker

A CLARIFICATION FROM PMO

Chairman, People's Welfare Suggestion Forum
Dt. 11.08.2024
Name Of Complainant- NANDA NANDAN DAS
Date of Receipt-11/08/2024
Received By Ministry/Department-Prime Minister's Office
Current Status-Case closed
Date of Action-12/08/2024
Reason-Others
Remarks-Thank you for your valuable suggestions.
Rating-Excellent
Remarks-Satisfied
Officer Concerns To
Officer Name-Mukul Dixit (Under Secretary (Public))
Organisation name-Prime Minister's Office
Contact Address-Public Wing 5th Floor, Rail Bhawan New Delhi
Email Address-us-public. sb@gov.in
Contact Number-011-23386447

Satisfied

CHAPTER XXII

THE KEY POINTS TO BRING BHARAT
- A DEVELOPED COUNTRY

Registration Number: PMOPG/E/2025/0001785

Dt. 04.01.2025

THE KEY POINTS TO BRING BHARAT - A DEVELOPED COUNTRY

Respected Shri Narendra Modi Ji, Hon'ble Prime Minister of India,

The following matter is submitted for your kind knowledge and further action towards achieving a developed Bharat in PDF format. These most important matters may kindly be perused, and action may be taken as deemed fit for the interest of the people and the growth of the nation.

With heartiest regards,

Yours sincerely,

Dr. Nanda Nandan Das, Original Thinker,

Former Secretary, Works Govt. of Odisha,

Chairman, People's Welfare Suggestion Forum

Dt. 04.01.2025

THE PDF ATTACHMENT –Dt. 03.01.2025

Respected Shri Narendra Modi Ji, Hon'ble Prime Minister of India,

The following matter is submitted for your kind knowledge and further action towards achieving a developed Bharat.

THE KEY POINTS TO BRING BHARAT - A DEVELOPED COUNTRY

More than seven decades have passed, yet our country remains a developing nation. Despite having the resources to achieve development within ten years, certain principles were not strictly adopted. However, there have been exceptional changes in the last decade.

To transform our country and states into developed entities, the universal solution (Copy right of Dr. Nanda Nandan Das) lies in NANDA'S SIX FORMULAE:

NANDA'S SIX FORMULAE: Vision, Target, Problems, Solutions, Programming to meet the target, Mode of achieving the vision.

1. VISION: To see a developed Bharat within 10 years.

2. TARGET: To develop the country within ten years by identifying all problems and finding suitable solutions to overcome them.

3. PROBLEMS: There is a lack of morality, unity, and national identity among the citizens, even after seven decades of independence. The citizens were mostly illiterate, with narrow feelings of religion, caste, socioeconomic status, and regional differences in pre-independence. No significant steps have been taken to minimize these differences, which are the main reasons for the lack of morality, unity, and national identity, hindering the country's development. To make our country developed, all lacunas, problems, retarding points, bottlenecks, and hindrances, which may be hundreds or thousands, need to be identified.

If the liability of a state is 1 lakh crore, then the state would be poor. However, if it has assets of 1 lakh crore, it would be a developed state. The same principle applies to a nation.

4. SOLUTIONS:

Proper governance is essential for generating a developed country or state. The government includes departmental heads, ministers, and concerned authorities. Unless these individuals possess 'Exceptional character'—honesty, sincerity, progressiveness, and creativity, good governance cannot be achieved. For example, China, despite being a communist country with a miserable situation in 1949, flourished due to the leadership of a top leader with exceptional character. Similarly, Dubai & Singapore, became a developed countries despite limited resources, including a scarcity of drinking water, due to exceptional leadership.

Presently, in our country, two leaders with exceptional character can be cited as examples: Shri Narendra Modi Ji, Hon'ble Prime Minister of India, and Shri Aditya Jogi Ji, Hon'ble Chief Minister of UP. Their exceptional character has led to rapid development in their respective areas. It is noted that the supporting staff and governance systems of these leaders are equally of exceptional character, making rapid progress and achievements possible.

At the time of independence, Pakistan (East & West) was separated from India to accommodate Muslim communities. Therefore, special Muslim status should not be a matter in this country. As Bharat is a country with a Hindu majority, the culture and heritage of Sanatan culture should be maintained. With Sanatan culture, all communities will stay safe and happy.

The solutions to each individual problem should be derived. There may be many, but the solution suitable to the situation should be made final. After identifying the exact solution to each problem, there will be no confusion on any issue.

The administration should ensure that there are assets instead of liabilities, which would be beneficial for development. Unnecessary subsidies for gaining votes are a significant drawback to development. Relief for the needy can be provided by the central government as a national scheme for all; no state should provide subsidies using public money. The Election Commission and central government should stop such promises that affect public property. If any relief is required specifically for a particular state, it should be agreed upon by both the state and central government, with a minimum of 60% of the funding coming from the central government and the rest from the state government.

5. PROGRAMMING TO ACHIEVE THE TARGET: After finalizing the solutions to all problems, a targeted timeline for the project's completion should be set, detailing its implementation.

6. MODE OF ACHIEVING THE VISION: The implementation procedure should then be followed as per the targeted time-bound program, ensuring the vision is achieved on time.

There are two ways to achieve ideal citizens and achieving developed county:

a. COMPULSORY INTRODUCTION OF MORAL VALUE IN EDUCATIONAL CURRICULUM

A course of moral science has been prepared for Class 1 to graduation, promoting the idea that all citizens are ideal Indians, irrespective of differences. This course has been suggested to the Hon'ble Prime Minister of India (registration number: PMOPG/E/2019/0640330) and all the Chief Ministers of the country. Implementing this course as a compulsory subject would generate Bharatiya with morality, unity, nationality, and ideal citizenship, irrespective of several differences. Citizens would possess 'Outstanding' (honest, sincere, and progressive) and 'Exceptional' (honest, sincere, progressive, and innovative) character. These terms are copyrighted by Dr. Nanda Nandan Das.

Common citizens would possess 'Outstanding' character, while top authorities such as political leaders would have 'Exceptional' character. With this grade of leadership, the country and states would develop, utilizing their resources efficiently. Countries like Japan, Norway, Sweden, Finland and many others, have developed due to leaders of Exceptional Character instilling moral values in the educational system.

b. STRONG ENFORCEMENT OF LAWS:

Countries like Dubai and Singapore have developed due to the strong enforcement of laws by their leaders. The present UP government is a typical example. Therefore, for our country, both methods are desirable and should be adopted without further delay. The posting of top authorities and ministers should be of

'Exceptional' character. Otherwise, the situation may deteriorate like in Bangladesh and Pakistan.

If required, old privileged rules that become bottlenecks for progress should be revised. Additionally, extra power should be granted to the police and government to ensure rapid and strong action on any issue. The case of the terrorist Ajmal Kasab, with all the proven crimes, took four years and incurred an expenditure of sixty crores before final conviction. This was not only time-consuming but also a huge budgetary loss to the country, a waste of public money, and an encouragement for more criminal activities. Therefore, all actions should be prompt and decisive.

NANDA'S SIX FORMULAE provide a pathway to a developed country and states, and can successfully address universal problems. By introducing moral values in the course of study, citizens of Outstanding and Exceptional Character will be generated. Exceptional (honest, sincere, progressive, and innovative) authorities and political leaders will form the best governance for the country's development. Similarly, strong enforcement of laws will ensure disciplined governance. For Bharat, both principles must be adopted to achieve early development.

CONCLUSION:

The following points should be deeply scrutinized with depth in feeling in sincerity and future planning for developed Bharat. It would be better if such matters in details, are to be brought to the knowledge of his kindness Hon'ble Prime Minister, Bharat.

* Moral Science should be a compulsory subject from Class 1 to graduation in all types of schools and colleges, based on the principle that all are ideal Indians, as suggested in registration number: PMOPG/E/2019/0640330 to the Hon'ble PM. Through such education, citizens of Outstanding and Exceptional Character would be created nationally.

* The highest authorities of government and ministers as heads of departments must be of 'Outstanding' character'. Postings should be made accordingly.

* The creation of assets for the states and the nation should be the main principle, and there should be accountability for creating liabilities for the states.

* Presently, it is seen that only Sanatan culture maintains universal peace through the concepts of 'Sarve Bhavantu Sukhinah' and 'Vasudhaiva Kutumbakam'. Such culture should prevail, and heritage must be maintained.

* The principle should be to raise the country's exchequer and improve the well-developed lifestyle for all.

* If required, laws should be reformed to suit present times, and the government should follow the rules strictly. The terrorism and crime should be strictly taken in to task.

* Nanda's Six Formulae should be followed to find solutions to any issue, no matter how critical it may be.

* Most religious disputes can be settled by directing individuals to observe their prayers in their respective houses and institutions peacefully, without disrupting common places. Any public gathering or procession on roads and in open places by any religious community should require permission from district authorities. As ideal Indians, all must maintain cordial, friendly relations and be helpful to each other, learning lessons from neighboring countries that suffer from poverty, crime, and terrorism, leading to restlessness. With warm regards,

Yours sincerely,

Dr. Nanda Nandan Das, Original Thinker

Former Secretary, Works Govt. of Odisha,

Chairman, People's Welfare Suggestion Forum

Dt. 03.01.2025

It was discussed in the special session of PWSF on 03.01.2024 in the office of People's Welfare Suggestion Forum at Baudpur, Bhadrak and was unanimously agreed upon to inform Hon'ble Prime Minister, Bharat to take step as suitable at his end.

The members present: Dr. Nanda Nandan Das, Er. Ambika Ballabh Swain, Er. Basanta Kumar Panigrahi, Gayadhar Panda, Akhoy Kumar Panda, Amiya Nanda Das, Ananta Narayana Panda, Goutam Das, Sk. Nasir Box, Amulya Prasad Naik, Basanta Kumar Mahanty, Bhagabat Mahallik, Shrikrishna Chaitanya Das.

Grievance Concerns to Name of Complainant
NANDA NANDAN DAS
Date of Receipt 04/01/2025
Received By Ministry/Department Prime Minister's Office
Grievance Document
Current Status Grievance Received
Date of Action 04/01/2025
Officer Concerns To
Forwarded to Prime Minister's Office
Officer Name Mukul Dixit, Under Secretary (Public)
Organisation name Prime Minister's Office
Contact Address-Public Wing 5th Floor, Rail Bhawan New Delhi
Email Address-us-public.sb@gov.in
Contact Number-011-23386447

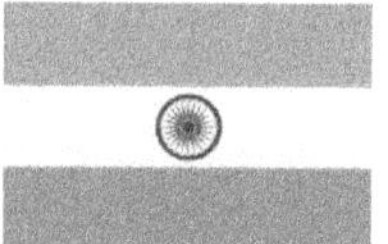

NARENDRA MODI, Prime Minister of India

CHAPTER XXXIII

THE PURSUIT OF TRUTH FOR GLOBAL PEACE ON MOTHER EARTH

NANDA NANDAN DAS

PEOPLE'S WELFARE SUGGESTION FORUM
COUNTRY FIRST

Regd. No.: 1567 / 2008 (Trust)
Bhubaneswar: Plot No. 2024, Chintamaniswar Colony, 751006, O
Bhadrak-Baudpur, P/S- Madhab Nagar, Dist. -Bhadrak, -756181
Ph.: 9437617604, 9437312986
Email: nandanandan_das@yahoo.com

Dt. 03.11.2024
To
The Hon'ble Members of the United Nations Security Council (UNSC)
Through: **His-Excellency Secretary-General, United Nations**
Subject: The Pursuit of Truth for Global Peace on Mother Earth

His-Excellency,
It has been observed that some nations are involved in activities that promote terrorism, war, and rivalry. This has led to widespread unrest on Earth, despite the fact that humanity is part of one global family. These issues arise from a mentality of territorial expansion, religious supremacy, egoism, self-interest, and monopolistic governance. Instead of fostering friendly relations, nations have turned to enmity. In truth, like all other living beings, humans are on this Earth for a finite time, and nothing truly belongs to them—not even their own bodies, souls, or breath.

THE TRUTH OF OUR EXISTENCE

Our universe began with a cosmic explosion, and the Sun, along with other stars, emerged. Scientific evidence suggests that Earth separated from the Sun about 4.5 billion years ago in burning state. The Earth's rotation on its axis forming day and night (Patent), the Moon's revolution around the Earth in a month (Patent), and the planet's magnetic field (Patent) were mysteries that have now been explored. Discoveries related to these phenomena have been documented and submitted for peer review by Dr. Nanda Nandan Das.

The separation of Earth from the Sun occurred due to a powerful force striking the Sun on its left side, causing a fragment to break away and move to a distance with an anti-clockwise rotation. During such process, a smaller part of the fragment was separated. The bigger part of fragment became Earth, while a smaller piece that separated became the Moon, revolving around the Earth.

Over billions of years, the Earth cooled, transitioning from a gaseous state to liquid (molten lava) and subsequently to solid crust. Water accumulated after temperature draw down below 100* C, and life began to emerge in water, on land, and in the air. Human-like creatures appeared over 100,000 years ago in Africa. These early humans, due to their advanced cognitive abilities, evolved socially and settled in Mesopotamia around 10,000 years ago as separate entity.

These early humans were nomadic but eventually spread across the globe, developing different languages, religions, and governance systems. Religious doctrines were adapted to suit regional communities, but in essence, humanity like all life on Earth, remains one community. Each individual's time on Earth is limited, and nothing truly belongs to anyone, not even their own existence.

Borders, languages, and religions are human-made constructs, created based on geography and circumstances. The COVID-19 pandemic demonstrated that these boundaries are artificial, as the virus knew no borders, and even religious institutions closed, becoming sources of its spread.

Unfortunately, some leaders, driven by ego, self-interest, an expansionist mindset, and a thirst for power, have disregarded the fundamental truths of life. This has led to conflict, terrorism, and destruction even at the expense of their own people and nations. The recent Hamas attack on Israel on October 7, 2023, is one such example. Though Israel suffered losses, most of the Hamas attackers were neutralized, leading to the near collapse of the group. Similarly, the ongoing war between Ukraine and Russia, now in its third year, has been intensified by external provocations, resulting in significant loss of life and widespread economic damage, affecting even their own countries.

Historical events, such as the First and Second World Wars and the atomic bombings in Japan, have caused untold suffering. In response, the United Nations was formed on October 24, 1945, with the five permanent members UK, USA, Russia, China, and France granted veto power. However, it was assumed that these countries would act in the greater interest of humanity, which has not always been the case.

CONCLUSION

1. All human beings belong to the Planet Earth of one global family. All should live well.
2. Since life is finite, we must work together to promote peace and harmony across all nations. It is good for all.
3. Religion is a personal, social bond. One should be free to practice the faith without disrupting others.
4. National leaders should serve as representatives of the United Nations, accountable for the welfare and development of their countries. Whatever small or big, the countries may be, the wellbeing of the people of the country would be look out of Country Heads.
5. The United Nations should control global defence systems to prevent conflicts.
6. Nuclear energy should be used for the exploration of space, controlling disaster management, and the welfare of humanity.
7. International discussions should prioritize the majority opinion for decision-making.
8. Education systems worldwide should adopt a value-based curriculum that promotes the idea of one human race, transcending all differences. Such value based educational curriculums, based on

all being tuned to ideal human had been sent to about heads of 170 countries through the book 'Moral Science' by Dr. Nanda Nandan Das.

9. Terrorism in all forms must be condemned and punished severely. The following concepts (Copy rights of Dr. N.N Das) should be universally accepted:

Gods: The Sun, Earth, and one's parents, as they sustain our existence.

Religion: Humanity is the true religion, as we are all part of one human race.

Caste: The only distinctions by birth are male and female, with equal rights for all.

The key points above aim to unify humanity and promote global peace.

These suggestions should be thoroughly reviewed and enhanced to pave the way for a united, peaceful world. We are grateful for your assistance.

With warm regards,

Yours sincerely,

Dr. Nanda Nandan Das, Original Thinker

Chairman, People's Welfare Suggestion Forum

03.11.2024

Members: Present on the debate: Dr. Nanda Nandan Das, Er. Ambika Ballabha Swain, Sri Goutam Das, Shri Arup Chand, Shri Ananta Narayan Panda, Shri Pramod Kumar Jena and Er. Kamala Kanta Behera.

FORWARDED TO DIFFERENT WORLD PEACE ORGANIZATIONS

NANDANANDAN DAS

To me, worldpeacefoundation@tufts.edu, World peace

Info, worldpeace@theowp.org, media@nobel.no, and more · Wed, Dec 11 at 8:10 PM

Respected Authority of the Institution,

I am forwarding the attached letter, addressed to the members of the UNSC through the Hon'ble Secretary-General of the UN on 23.11.2024, for your information and necessary action. This is in pursuit of truth for global peace on Mother Earth. The letter contains solutions to achieve global peace, and the matter is self-explanatory.

With warm regards,

Yours sincerely,

Dr. Nanda Nandan Das, Original Thinker,

Chairman, People's Welfare Suggestion Forum. State-Odisha, India

Phone: +91 9437617604

Email: nandanandan_das@yahoo.com

Dt.11.12.2024